Recreditpair!

Recreditpair!

A Complete Guide to Understanding and Improving Your Credit

JIM LONGACRE

Kele
PUBLISHING

KELE PUBLISHING
P.O. Box 1327
Placerville, CA 95667

© by Jim Longacre
Cover and interior design by Vanessa Perez
All rights reserved, including the right of reproduction in whole or in part in any form.
First Kele Publishing Edition 2008

For information regarding special discounts for bulk purchases, please call 1-800-581-0520

10 9 8 7 6 5 4 3 2 1

The Library of Congress Cataloguing-in-Publication Data is pending
Jim Longacre

       Recreditpair/ Jim Longacre—Re. ed;1st Kele Publishing ed.
p.   cm.
1.   Credit—repair—United States. 2. Personal financial—self-help—United States
1.Title
       DNLM: 1. Credit—education—Financial self-help. 2. Finance—credit repair. 3. Self-help—fixing your credit. 4. Financial self-help—credit repair.
Txul pending

ISBN:0-9762931-1-0   0

Printed in Canada

Recreditpair! is dedicated to my three sons, Jason, Garrett, and Travis, and to everyone seeking financial independence through better credit.

CONTENTS

ACKNOWLEDGMENTS

I would like to thank some very special people in my life, who inspired, pushed and otherwise encouraged me to write this book. Without their support, Recreditpair may have ended up an unrealized dream, and those whom it helps would not have been able to gain the financial independence they deserve.

My special thanks to: Elizabeth Clark, Jason Longacre, Garrett Longacre, Travis Longacre, Karrie Miller, Kolton Miller, Chadders, Bill W., Max the Dog, Mitz the Cat, and my biggest historical hero, Abraham Lincoln.

There were many working colleagues who played important roles in helping to develop this book, as well as taking part in our other projects and I would like to thank them for their fine talents and relentless enthusiasm, and may we share many more projects to come! Thanks to: John Linton, Kent Emmons, Johnathan Flicker, Michael Bowker, Brad Hirsch, Kurt Bujack, James and Leslie Simz, Andy Ross, John Arvanitis, Brandon Contreras, David Bruni, Tom Coshow, and Sarah Fennema.

INTRODUCTION

Chances are that if you're reading this book you have seen me talking about *Recreditpair* in one of hundreds of live seminars I've conducted in person, on television, or over the Internet. It really doesn't matter. What does matter is that you are ready and willing to use this book to take the steps necessary to gain control of your credit profile. I commend you for that because many people are too intimidated to begin the journey toward better credit. Working to improve your credit can be a daunting task – until you learn how to do it! You've already taken the first step by purchasing this book. The rest is simply a matter of following the easy-to-understand steps I provide here. Because you are willing to do this, you are already on the road toward changing your life in many positive ways! Believe me, your hard work will not go unrewarded.

One of the reasons I decided to write this book and help people repair and strengthen their credit is that I once struggled through credit problems myself. When I was young and people asked me what I wanted to do when I grew up, I'm pretty sure I never said, "When I become an adult, I want to have credit problems!" Unfortunately, though, that is exactly what happened to me.

A series of misfortunes, some my fault and others not, led me into personal bankruptcy in 1992. I was devastated. I lost my home, automobiles, credit cards, self-esteem, and pride. I gained a lot of shame and confusion. I had no one to guide me. I couldn't buy a house or get a decent price on anything. My first car after the bankruptcy was a 1991 Ford Tempo that I purchased at 28 percent interest. At that point, I was grateful just to have a car, but I knew I was paying an enormous financial price for the right to borrow money with bad credit. I also knew I had to do whatever it took to rebuild my credit. I knew I couldn't afford to be credit poor!

I began studying every possible avenue back to good credit. I read everything I could lay my hands on about re-establishing better credit. I talked to lenders, brokers, and financial experts and attended numerous seminars on the subject. I focused especially on the lending requirements for mortgages and vehicles. Over the next few years, I watched my credit scores improve and eventually was pleased to find myself paying normal interest rates and fees. In addition, I had learned so much about repairing credit that people began to seek my advice and assistance. I was happy to help them. Finally, in 1998, I began to give free credit-repair seminars.

At the time, credit-repair companies were coming into vogue, and I thought I could improve the quality of my seminars by inviting representatives of local credit-repair companies to attend. It soon became evident that these companies weren't all they were cracked up to be. As they began to compete for clients, they made outlandish statements about what they could do to solve credit problems. Each one claimed to have a "secret," and some of them charged outlandish fees for their work. It didn't take long for me to realize that I was already teaching their "secrets" in my seminars, and I quit inviting them to participate. The truth is that few credit-repair companies provide services that you cannot provide for yourself by following the advice in this book. The credit-repair companies have turned a good idea into a rip-off, and now we need to get back to basics.

Encouraged by the success that my seminar attendees had in improving their credit, I put all of my ideas down on paper (and onto a CD) and called it *Recreditpair*. I wanted to create a tool for success that anyone could use. *Recreditpair* contains a set of clear instructions and gives access to resources that will turn you into your own credit-repair company. This book will help you understand, improve, and maintain your credit for life. You can also help your friends and family improve their credit.

I'm going to say something that at first might seem a little strange. That is, all the information and processes described in *Recreditpair* are merely suggestions. Let me explain what I mean. At my seminars, I ask my audiences if anyone has ever skydived. In a memorable moment at a seminar in Sacramento, California, a man with a cast on his leg raised his crutch and shouted, "I have!" His response to my question gave me the idea for the following allegory. Assume you are skydiving, and when you jump out of the airplane you see the word "pull" printed on your parachute next to the ripcord. Now, you must understand that the word is just a suggestion. You really don't have to pull the cord that opens your chute, but it's a good idea if you do. The same is true of the instructions contained in this book. They are only suggestions, but they are designed to improve your life and keep you and your family from experiencing a rough financial landing. I know you will benefit from the suggestions in this book. I would wish you good luck, but with *Recreditpair* and your own determination to NEVER GIVE UP, you won't need luck. You can improve your credit scores. Finish reading this book, and I'll see you in the land of good credit!

Best wishes,

Jim Longacre

February 3, 2008
Citrus Heights, California

PART I

PART I

The *Recreditpair* Process

Steps Necessary to Make Your Credit Report Accurate:

- Obtain Your Credit Reports
- Review and Understand Your Credit Reports
- Dispute All Inaccurate or Questionable Information
- Negotiate With Collection Companies
- Establish New Accounts
- Pay Current Accounts on Time
- Review the Responses to Your Disputes
- Re-dispute Inaccurate or Questionable Accounts That Were Not Deleted
- Never Give Up

Good Credit —
It's More Important than Ever!

The goal of *Recreditpair* is to simplify the complexities of the secret world of credit — made secret by those who want to make it difficult for people to improve their credit scores. Specifically, I'm talking about the lenders that control the credit-reporting agencies (also known as credit bureaus) and that benefit from consumers' having lower credit scores than they should. This book provides you with the tools to obtain, understand, raise, and maintain your own credit score. You may have read a little about this in the past and have been overwhelmed by the mountain of information that the author placed before you. Most of the books I've read on credit repair contain a lot of material that isn't relevant to gaining control of your credit and are so confusing that they probably stop many people from trying. I intend to avoid that here.

Recreditpair is designed to make understanding and improving your credit fast and easy. The steps listed above cut through this mountain of confusion and serve as the foundation for your actions. Once you have mastered these simple steps, you will be well on your way toward managing your credit for life. That's all there is to it! It seems easy enough, but you must have patience, because the credit-reporting agencies are not always cooperative. Their profits come from selling information and not from correcting inaccurate records.

Although most of us think we know intuitively what "credit" is in terms of our financial present and future, it's important to consider, for a moment, all the nuances of what the term really means. Credit is more than simply your ability to obtain a loan at a good interest rate. It is based on your reputation as a person of sound character and is rooted in your past financial behavior. Good credit means you are a person who can be trusted as a borrower. It indicates that you are true to your word when you promise to maintain a schedule of payments to a lender over a period of time. Your credit status says a lot about you as a person, and this book will help you ensure that what it says is accurate.

Before going further, let me underscore how important good credit is to our lives. Most of you already know that good credit can help you make major purchases, such as houses and automobiles. Much more, however, rides on your credit scores. Here's a look at some of the major ways credit impacts your life:

- Over your lifetime, the difference between good credit and mediocre credit can mean hundreds of thousands of dollars in your pocket. **Some experts estimate that mediocre-to-poor credit can cause YOU TO PAY MORE THAN $300,000 during your lifetime than you would if you had good credit scores.** The extra costs come in the form of higher interest rates and extra fees on auto loans, mortgages, credit cards, bank loans, and other types of financing. This estimate does not include the additional hundreds of thousands of dollars you might have generated by wisely investing the money you saved by having good credit. When I say that good credit is worth a fortune, I mean it!

- Prospective employers often check credit scores before deciding whether or not to hire someone. In our society, the financial world equates good credit with good character. Conversely, if you have bad credit, you are considered a risk and perhaps irresponsible, and if your credit score is lower than it should be, that preconception might prevent you from landing a good job.

- Even if you choose to rent an apartment rather than purchase a house, poor credit can harpoon your efforts. Most landlords routinely check your credit, and an unfavorable credit report can cause you to be turned down even for a rental unit.

- Homeowners-insurance companies and life-insurance carriers also look closely at credit reports. Some carriers deny coverage to applicants with bad credit.

- Bad credit can also get in the way of achieving other goals. Perhaps the most important goal is building and maintaining a good relationship with your spouse or significant other. Finances ignite many marital battles, and if you are single, you might find that someone you

like a lot loses interest in you because your poor credit situation indicates that you will not make a sound
financial partner.

I could list myriad other ways that credit affects our
lives, but I think you get the point. Good credit is essential
to maintaining a productive and healthy lifestyle. Now, let's
find out how to get it and keep it!

PART II

PART II

Your Credit and You

An Overview of the Credit Industry

Three major credit-reporting agencies dominate the credit industry and provide your all-important credit scores. Over the past few decades, these three agencies have risen quietly to become, like it or not, vitally important in our lives. Through this book, you'll get to know more about them and how you can best interact with them to get what you need most—good credit scores. The three agencies are:

Equifax
P.O. Box 740241
Atlanta, GA 30374-0241
800-525-6285
www.equifax.com

Experian

National Consumers Assistance Center

P.O. Box 2104

Allen, TX 75013-2104

888-397-3742

www.experian.com

TransUnion

Consumer Disclosure Center

P.O. Box 2000

Chester, PA 19022-2000

800-916-8800

www.transunion.com

These companies are like mechanized monsters that in many ways control our financial lives. In truth, though, they are little more than databases that collect information from creditors such as credit-card companies, banks, mortgage companies, and other entities that lend money. The information they collect is compiled to create your individual credit report, which seems innocuous enough, until you begin to understand how powerfully they can affect your ability to reach your financial dreams.

In a nutshell, here is how it works. Your completion of a credit application for a loan to purchase a product or service usually generates a credit inquiry. This credit inquiry, whether submitted by a local automobile dealership from which you seek a car loan or by a mortgage company from which you seek a real-estate loan, is displayed on your credit report along with other information about you, including your payment history and public records, such as tax liens, bankruptcies, and judgments. It may surprise you to learn that having too many inquiries on your credit report can harm your credit score, but I'll discuss that in greater detail later in the book. The point is that your ability to obtain a loan and to get a good interest rate on it depends on the information that appears on your credit report. This brings us to the first critical point. It is essential that you ensure that ALL of the information displayed on your credit reports is accurate. *ESTIMATES INDICATE THAT AS MANY AS 80 PERCENT OF ALL CREDIT REPORTS CONTAIN INACCURACIES!* In this book, I'll show you how to correct information on your credit report that is inaccurate or dated.

The *Recreditpair* System

As I move forward with my explanation of the *Recreditpair* method, you will learn how to:

- understand your credit reports,
- dispute any questionable information, and
- correspond with the three major credit-reporting agencies.

The Letter Generator included in the *Recreditpair* software will help you create the appropriate letters for corresponding with the major credit-reporting agencies about information that they post to your credit file and use to calculate your credit score. Alternatively, you can use the sample letters as a resource for creating your own customized letters. The *Recreditpair* software system automatically addresses letters to any of the three credit-repair agencies with just a push of a button. The system also automatically creates file copies to help you stay organized. You can order the *Recreditpair* software system by calling 1-800-851-6686.

What is a Credit Score?

Okay, let's get down to it. What is a credit score? Essentially, it is an attempt by the credit-reporting agencies (credit bureaus) to evaluate how much risk you represent to a potential lender by giving you a credit score that is based on all the financial information that the credit bureaus can obtain about you. This information is then put into a complex mathematical model that shakes and bakes it, and then bingo—out comes your credit score! The models the credit bureaus use are far from perfect, however, and mistakes are commonplace, which is why you must examine the information in the database to ensure that your creditworthiness is being evaluated fairly.

Once the credit-reporting agencies calculate your credit score, lenders use it to help determine whether you qualify for credit cards, loans, or services. The point of the scoring is to assist lenders in determining the likelihood that you will make payments on time. Generally, the higher the credit score, the lower the risk. Lenders and employers use your credit score to anticipate the risk you pose when they do business with you; insurance companies use it to estimate how likely you are to have accidents or to file claims; employers use it to help determine your desirability as a potential employee, and landlords use it to determine whether you are likely to pay the rent on time. Keep in mind that the credit-reporting agencies calculate your credit scores principally for the benefit of lenders. Thus, credit scores are not consumer-friendly; they are designed to protect creditors.

Each of the credit-reporting agencies collects information provided by businesses that have an interest in extending credit to members of the public. This information includes the date the account was opened, payment history, open balances, and type of account. The account types include home loans, automobile loans, utility bills, credit cards, department-store purchases, and other accounts that require timely payments. The rating system is designed to produce a score between 350 and 850.

According to estimates, missing one payment to a major lender can subtract from 40 to 100 points from your credit score. A big event, like a bankruptcy, can knock 200 points or more off your credit score.

Each credit-reporting agency employs a unique method for calculating credit scores. Thus, using the same information, their resulting credit scores can differ by as much as 50 points. This discrepancy can be frustrating for individuals, but the credit-reporting agencies are all trying to do the same thing—determine the potential risk you represent to the lender. Other information about you is contained in your credit reports as well, including current and previous addresses, date of birth, employment history, homeownership status, and income level. Other areas of your report provide records of creditors who have requested your credit history within the past year and of employers who have requested your credit history for employment purposes during the past two years.

Your report also includes a public-records section that includes judgments, foreclosures, bankruptcies, and tax liens. Filing any of these with a court will generate an entry on your credit report.

How Credit Scoring is Used

One of the primary ways your credit score is used is to determine which loan category you will be assigned. Believe me, it makes a big difference which of these you get. The three major loan categories are Prime, Sub-Prime, and Below Sub-Prime. An explanation of each follows:

1) **Prime**: If your credit score is 680 or above, you are considered a "prime" borrower and will have few problems getting a good interest rate on your home loan, car loan, or credit card. You will also pay lower fees and be able to negotiate other favorable terms. THIS IS THE LOAN CATEGORY YOU WANT!

2) Sub-Prime: If your credit score falls from 560 to 679, you are considered a "sub-prime" borrower and will likely pay higher interest rates on your loans. In the past few years, lenders dipped into the sub-prime markets and aggressively marketed shaky loans that offered seductively low near-term interest rates that escalate dramatically after a few years. These loans lured people into buying homes they could not afford and helped fuel the present credit crisis.

3) Below Sub-Prime: A credit score of 559 or below presents the worst of the three scenarios. If your credit score falls into this category, I suggest that we work together to get you out of it as soon as possible. Sure, you can still obtain credit cards, but you will likely be hit with security deposits or high acquisition fees. In addition, your interest rates may be over 20 percent! Ouch! Obtaining home mortgages or automobile loans with a score below 560 is also difficult. Even if you succeed in securing a loan with such a low score, you will almost certainly pay a high interest rate and additional fees. Many insurance companies charge higher premiums depending on your credit score. Additionally, a low score may prevent you from getting a job with many companies.

The Origins of the Monster

Credit-reporting agencies and credit scoring are relatively recent phenomena. In 1956, Bill Fair and Earl Isaac founded the Fair Isaac firm, which has become synonymous with credit reporting. Fair, an engineer, and Isaac, a mathematician, felt that they could design a mathematical formula that would help lenders predict how much risk a potential borrower represents. Being analytical types, they wanted to create a model that would eliminate the biases of the lenders and replace them with hard economic facts. Before long, Fair Isaac grew to dominate the world of credit reporting, and the credit score swiftly became a cornerstone of the financial status of nearly every working American. The monster was loose and unstoppable. Along the way, the credit-information process became secretive and some say distorted. Sometimes those not familiar with the history of credit scoring see the name Fair Isaac and think of "fair" as an adjective that describes the credit-scoring industry. It is not! Often, credit scoring is anything but fair. You must work to make it so. Credit reports often contain inaccuracies, and the process for getting them corrected may seem quite unjust. While our justice system considers an accused person innocent until proven guilty, our credit-reporting system presumes guilt and requires you to prove your innocence!

Credit reporting and credit scores have become increasingly important in our lives because we utilize credit as

never before. From 1990 to 2000, amounts extended to debtors through credit cards, automobile loans, and non-mort-
gage credit doubled to more than $1.7 trillion. Home-equity
loans rocketed to more than $1 trillion in 2003. That's a lot
of credit, and its approval depended largely on credit scores!
The monster created by Bill Fair and Earl Isaac has become
bigger than they could have imagined. Unfortunately, it's
loose, and we must deal with it.

What's a FICO Score?

The three largest credit-reporting agencies do not directly decide your creditworthiness. Rather, lenders such as banks and
credit-card companies do so. They report the information to the
credit-reporting agencies. The agencies, however, are far from
being innocent bystanders in the fight for good credit. They
make frequent mistakes and are often frightfully sloppy and
careless when it comes to the maintenance of your credit score.
Fortunately, the law requires them to clean up their errors. In
order to get their attention, though, you have to point out those
errors to them in writing. I'll cover this later in greater detail.

FICO® is the credit score with which most people are familiar. This credit-scoring formula, which is the most widely
used and the most important, was developed by the Fair Isaac
firm and is employed by TransUnion. The exact algorithm or
formula is secret, but FICO has been around long enough for
us to draw some conclusions about how it operates. FICO is
used in billions of lending decisions each year, including 75
percent of the mortgage-lending assessments.

Factors that Make up Your Credit Score:

The five factors that are used to calculate your credit score are:

1. **PAYMENT HISTORY (35%).** Late payments have a huge negative effect on your credit score. You should vow right now to pay your credit-card and other bills on time. If late payments appear on your credit report, your credit score will suffer. Bankruptcies and delinquent accounts sent to collection or charged off as uncollectible are damaging to your financial well-being. The most recently recorded information has the greatest effect on your credit, while information over two years old has less of an impact.

2. **DEBT IN USE (30%).** You should be aware of the limits on your credit card or other loans, because 30 percent of your credit score is based on the ratio between how much you owe on your credit cards and other loans and their credit limits. The credit bureaus will penalize you for excessive debt in use. In other words, owing $5,500 on a credit card that has a limit of $6,000 counts against you and lowers your credit score. *Even running up only one of your accounts to near its limit can hurt your score.* You should keep your credit-card balances below 30 percent of the available limits. For example, if you have a credit card with a $1,000 limit, you should pay the balance down to under $300 dollars every month.

3. **LENGTH OF YOUR CREDIT HISTORY (15%).** Ideally, your accounts should be open for more than two years with no late payments. Sometimes, you must have at least three accounts open for more than a year to obtain a credit score.

4. **RECENT INQUIRIES (10%).** Credit-reporting agencies become nervous when you suddenly get interested in lots of new credit. Applying for many new accounts will negatively affect your credit score. Promotional inquiries do not count. Although inquiries remain on your report for up to two years, those made in the last six months count most heavily against you. If you have a number of recent inquiries on your credit report, though, you need not panic. Time passes quickly, and you can begin to build a better credit score now!

5. **TYPES OF CREDIT IN USE (10%).** The three major types of loans are used for credit cards (unsecured), mortgages (secured), and automobiles (secured). In an ideal-credit-score scenario, you would have a mortgage, an automobile loan, and three credit cards. If you are unable to purchase a home or automobile right now, however, you need not worry. This factor comprises is only ten percent of your credit score, and not having these types of loans will not destroy your ability to get good credit.

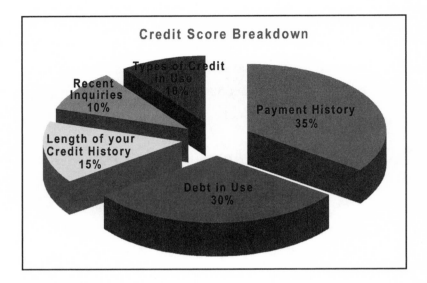

Your Legal Rights

Even though the credit industry's decision-making deck seems to be stacked against you, you do have a number of rights under the law. The Fair Isaac firm was responsible, in large part, for the secrecy that permeates the credit-scoring process. At one point, Congress felt that consumers were being abused, so it passed the Fair Credit Reporting Act (FCRA) to promote accuracy, fairness, and privacy of information in the files of every credit-reporting agency.

Most credit-reporting agencies gather and sell information about consumers to creditors, employers, landlords, and other businesses. You can find the complete text of the FCRA, 15 U.S.C. §§ 1681-681u, at the Federal Trade Commission's website (www.ftc.gov). You can find additional information at www.ftc.gov/credit, or you can write to:

Consumer Response Center
Room 130-A
Federal Trade Commission
600 Pennsylvania Avenue N.W.
Washington, D.C. 20580.

Here is a summary of your major rights under the FCRA.

- You must be told if information in your file has been used against you. Anyone who uses your credit report or other type of consumer report to deny your application for credit, insurance, or employment (or to take other adverse action against you) must tell you so. They must also give you the name, address, and telephone number of the credit-reporting agency that provided the information.

- You have a right to know what is in your file. You may request and obtain all the information compiled by the credit-reporting agencies. This is called a "file disclosure." To obtain a file disclosure, you'll need to provide proper identification, which may include your social-security number. In many cases, credit-reporting agencies must provide file disclosures free of charge.

You are entitled to a free file disclosure if:

- A person or company has taken adverse action against you because of information in your credit report;

- You are the victim of identify theft and place a fraud alert in your file;

- Identity theft or fraud caused inaccurate information to be reflected in your file;

- You are unemployed and state that you intend to apply for employment within 60 days, or

- You rely on public assistance.

You are entitled to one free file disclosure every twelve months from each credit bureau. You must request it in writing. You should not be timid about requesting your credit score; you have a right to do so under the law.

You may request your credit score from credit-reporting agencies that create credit scores or distribute them for use in residential real-estate loans, but you will have to pay for it. In many mortgage transactions, though, you will receive free credit-score information from the mortgage lender.

Remember, you are in charge of your own credit score. You have a right to dispute incomplete or inaccurate information, and you should make a habit of doing so. The law is on your side. **If you identify information in your credit report that is incomplete or inaccurate and report it to the credit-reporting agency, the agency must investigate your dispute.** The law states that credit-reporting agencies must correct or delete inaccurate, incomplete, or unverifiable information. Normally, erroneous entries must be removed or corrected within 30 days, but a credit-reporting agency may continue to report information it verifies as accurate. Also, these agencies may not report outdated negative information. In most cases, a credit-reporting agency may not report negative information that is more than seven years old or bankruptcies that are more than ten years old.

Summary

By now, you are beginning to get a clearer picture of your legal rights and what you need to do to boost your credit score to its highest possible level. Having an accurate credit report is a critical component to creating a sound financial future. A few late payments can cost you dearly. Banks and credit-card companies will charge you more if you have a low credit score, and you may pay higher auto-insurance and life-insurance premiums, as well. Utility companies often review credit reports prior to connecting their services. You may even be prevented from opening a bank account if you have less-than-stellar credit. Finally, many prospective employers review credit reports to determine character. The details in your report can weigh heavily on their decision to hire you.

If you diligently use the information contained in this book, you will achieve the best credit score possible. Let's march forward, then, with our review of how *Recreditpair* can assist you in taking control of your credit.

PART III

PART III

The Credit-Improvement Process

How to Obtain Your Credit Report

As I mentioned earlier, three major credit-reporting agencies dominate the credit-reporting industry—Experian, Equifax, and TransUnion. Each of these credit bureaus calculates its credit scores differently. As a result, it is important to obtain a credit report from each of them.

You can obtain one free credit report each year by visiting www.annualcreditreport.com. In order to get the most out of the *Recreditpair* process, however, I recommend that you obtain your credit report every 30-60 days during the first year. This allows you to monitor your progress and verify that creditors are removing inaccurate items. You cannot move forward with *Recreditpair* until you receive your credit reports. Simply click on the first link titled "Obtain" in the *Recreditpair* software system.

From there, you will be able to print your credit report directly from your computer. Always print a copy of your credit report. You will need to make multiple copies when you begin to draft letters. You should include a copy of your credit report showing the items you are disputing with every letter you send.

To obtain your credit report, you'll need the following information:

- Your social-security number;
- Your current and former home addresses and the dates you lived at each location;
- Your credit-card-account numbers, and
- Your other loan-account numbers.

Reading and Understanding Your Credit Report

You are not alone if you feel that credit reports can appear confusing and intimidating. Believe me, this is not accidental. The more difficult the information is to decipher, the more control the credit-reporting agencies (and creditors) have over consumers. With a bit of patience, however, you can read your credit report. For example, all credit reports include a "trade line" for each creditor. A trade line is simply a line or column of information on your credit report. Fortunately, once you understand how to read and interpret a single trade line, understanding all trade lines becomes easy.

Listed below are credit-report tips and examples of the most important credit-report sections. We shall concentrate on the "Merged Credit Report," which includes combined details from Experian, Equifax, and TransUnion. Single credit reports are issued by only one of the credit-report agencies and contain only the information reported to that specific agency.

After you obtain your credit report, look it over carefully for mistakes. If you find some, don't worry; they can be corrected. Note that the reports from each of the credit bureaus vary slightly in appearance. All of the reports contain the same basic information, but while one report may contain errors, another may be completely clean. You must carefully check all three agencies' reports.

The most important thing to check is your personal information, such as your name, address, date of birth, and social-security number. It isn't unusual for another person's information to show up on your credit report, even if you have no knowledge of or dealings with this person. Such mistakes are common, so be sure to pay special attention to this part.

The Four Critical Areas of Your Report

In this section, I shall focus on the following critical areas of your credit report: personal information, open and closed accounts, public records, and inquiries.

Report Date: 07/02/06

Sam

This is your Personal Info Section with your Social Security#, past and current Employment, Address and Report #. Check for errors here first!

1 **Consumer Informati**

Experian

Name:	John Jones
Report Acct #:	xxx-xxx-xxx
SSN:	XXX-XX-XX
Current Address:	555 Town S
Previous Address:	100 Orange
Current Employer:	ACME Mfg.
Previous Employer:	Corporate M

You have the option of adding a 100 word or less Statement to your Credit Report.

2 **Consumer Statemen**

I did not make the payment to ABC Electronics because
replace the radio and they would not let me return or ex

There are 5 types of accounts displayed in your Summary.
1) Installment
2) Revolving
3) Real Estate
4) Other
5) Collection

3 **Summary Informati**

Real Estate Accounts	**Experia**
Count	1
Balance	$79,000.0
Payment	$965.00
Current	1
Delinquent	0
Derogatory	0
Unknown	0
Revolving Accounts	**Experia**
Count	2
Balance	$1326.00

↓ **More Details can be found below**

redit Report

our Personal Information is tracked for 7 years

TransUnion	Equifax
John Jones	John Jones
xxx-xxx-xxxxxx	xxx-xxx-xxxxxx
XXX-XX-XXXX	XXX-XX-XXXX
555 Town St., Denver,CO	555 Town St., Denver,CO
100 Orange Ct., Chicago, IL	100 Orange Ct., Chicago, IL
ACME Mfg.	ACME Mfg.
Corporate Mfg.	Corporate Mfg.

t was delivered in defective condition. ABC Electronics would not repair or
Since the radio was defective and un-useable I refused to pay for it.

TransUnion	Equifax
1	1
$79,000.00	$79,000.00
$965.00	$965.00
1	1
1	0
0	0
0	0

TransUnion	Equifax
3	3
$1275.00	$1326.00

Note the slight differences between the Account Balances

After verifying your personal information, you should review both your open accounts and your closed accounts to ensure that they are correct. Then continue with the first reading of your credit report with the goal of identifying potentially inaccurate or negative items, such as tax liens, bankruptcies, judgments, lawsuits, late payments, collections, charge-offs, and repossessions.

Most of your financial history, including the names of your creditors, appears on your credit report. You should carefully read this section and search for errors. If you find problems, highlight them with a marker, especially if they are inaccurate or unverifiable and reflect negatively on your report. These items are the accounts you will dispute with the credit agencies. I'll talk more about how to do that in a minute.

Keep in mind that the law requires that the credit-reporting agencies explain anything on your credit report that you do not understand. You should contact them if you are confused about any entry on your credit report. At the top of the section that contains the account information is a legend that identifies the information contained in each column. First, you should highlight all negative information, including listings you feel are questionable, incomplete, or unverifiable.

1. **"Questionable"** items are those that contain inconsistencies, errors in reporting time, conflicting information, and so forth. You should pursue the correction of these items with your creditors. If they are inaccurate, you can dispute them and get them changed.

2. **"Incomplete"** items are often the most difficult to identify because they are usually errors of omission. For example, the accounts listed on your credit reports may not show an updated payment history or may not include accurate reporting of all the details included in the trade line.

3. **"Unverifiable"** items are ones that cannot be shown to belong to you. For example, if a company goes out of business, it can no longer verify its information. If the information negatively affects your credit score, you can request that it be removed from your credit report. Creditors must be able to prove that all information in their trade line is accurate. If they are unable to do so, the credit-reporting agencies should remove the corresponding trade lines from the report. Remember, the negatives contained in your credit reports are allegations made against you by your creditors; they are not official government statements. You have a right to challenge their accuracy. Once challenged, your creditors must prove that these negative items are correct. If they cannot do so, the credit-reporting agencies must remove the account from your credit reports.

Your right to dispute incomplete or inaccurate credit-report information is protected by the Fair Credit Reporting Act (FCRA). The FRCA puts significant power in your hands. You can dispute information that you feel is inaccurate or incomplete, including errors involving bankruptcies, late payments, collections, write-offs, liens, foreclosures, and repossessions.

Understanding Your Credit Report

The Personal-Information Section

I've already covered this, but I want to add that this section should include the date the information was first reported to the credit bureau by your creditors and the date it was last updated.

The Consumer-Statement Section

This section is voluntary and allows you to submit a 100-word explanation of a disputed claim to the credit-reporting agency for full viewing by any lender checking your report. You should not do this unless it's necessary. Sometimes, fighting unnecessary battles draws unwanted attention to a negative event. If you have a serious dispute, however, and it would look bad on your credit report or perhaps already negatively affects your credit score, then you might write a statement explaining your disagreement with the creditor regarding the amount owed on an account.

IMPORTANT NOTE: YOU SHOULD ONLY SUBMIT A CONSUMER STATEMENT AS A LAST RESORT.

The Summary-Information Section

The Summary-Information Section contains your payment history broken down by account type. The five account types, some of which overlap, are:

- **Real-Estate Account**: This generally refers to primary and secondary mortgages on your home.

- **Revolving Accounts**: These accounts have varying terms and payment schedules and include credit-card accounts.

- **Installment Accounts**: These are loans with fixed terms and regular payments, such as automobile loans. Real-estate mortgages with fixed-interest rates also can fall into this category.

- **Other Accounts**: These are accounts that do not fit into precise categories and might include 30-day accounts, such as an American-Express® account.

- **Collection Accounts**: As you may have guessed, these are accounts that are seriously past due. They may have been assigned to an attorney, a collection agency, or a creditor's internal-collection department. You should avoid them like the plague.

The following terms and information apply to all five account types. I have attempted to simplify the jargon for you.

- **Count:** This is financial shorthand for the total number of accounts you have in a loan category.

- **Balance:** This is the total amount you owe on all of your accounts in a category.

- **Payment:** This is the total of the monthly payments you must make on all accounts in a category.

- **Current:** This is the total number of accounts for which your payments are current.

- **Delinquent:** This refers to the number of accounts in a category for which you have been late on a payment. You should try for a zero in this category.

- **Derogatory or Adverse:** This represents the total number of accounts in a category that are damaging your credit rating. It is a critical number for you to scrutinize.

- **Unknown:** This category lists the number of accounts that the credit-reporting agency cannot verify. Having accounts in this category can work against you. When the unknown accounts are current and you have been paying your bills on time, you would expect a positive, or at least neutral, effect on your credit score. Instead, you lose your good karma because the agency cannot verify the account, and your credit score goes down. You should closely examine this section for errors. In it, you may find open accounts, closed accounts, public records, or inquiries.

- **Open/Closed Accounts**: This lists your accounts that are either open or closed.

- **Public Records**: These are public records that appear under your name, to include judgments against you, tax liens, and bankruptcies. This entry also includes the total dollar amount of all liabilities represented by your public-record items.

- **Inquiries**: An inquiry appears on your record when an organization, such as a bank or retail store, requests a copy of your credit report. Credit-reporting agencies generally look at how many inquiries were made on your credit report within the past two years.

The Account-History-Information Section

As you might expect, this section contains information about your credit history, including activities involving your credit accounts. It also includes other information, such as lawsuits, judgments, collections, and other matters that involve your accounts. The summary ratings for each account

4 **Account History Informa**

Creditor Name
ACME Mortgage   **Experian**

Account #	xxx-xxxx-xxx
Type:	Real Estate
Condition:	Open
Responsibity:	Individual
Pay Status:	60 days late
Date Opened:	07/01/05
Date Reported:	02/01/06
Balance and Limits:	$79,000.00
Payment and Terms:	$965.00 for 360 m
High Balance:	$84,000.00
Past Due:	$0
Remarks:	

This is the Creditor Info for a Home Mortgage Loan from ACME Mortgage

Two Year Payment History:

Experian   CUR CUR CUR CUR CUR CUR CUR CUR
           Aug Sep Oct Nov Dec Jan Feb Ma

TransUnion CUR CUR CUR CUR CUR CUR CUR CUR
           Aug Sep Oct Nov Dec Jan Feb Ma

Equifax   CUR CUR CUR CUR CUR CUR CUR CUR
           Aug Sep Oct Nov Dec Jan Feb Ma
                                      2005

Look for "Past Dues" and compare to your Records to find Report Errors

Seven Year Payment History:
                              Experian

30 Days Late:	1
60 Days Late:	1
90 Days Late:	0
120 Days Late:	0
150 Days Late:	0
Charge Off:	0

Later in this Chapter we will compose a Dispute Letter regarding Errors in January

A "Ch is the wo as this m Account in Coll

Legend   CUR = CURRENT
              = 120 DAYS LA

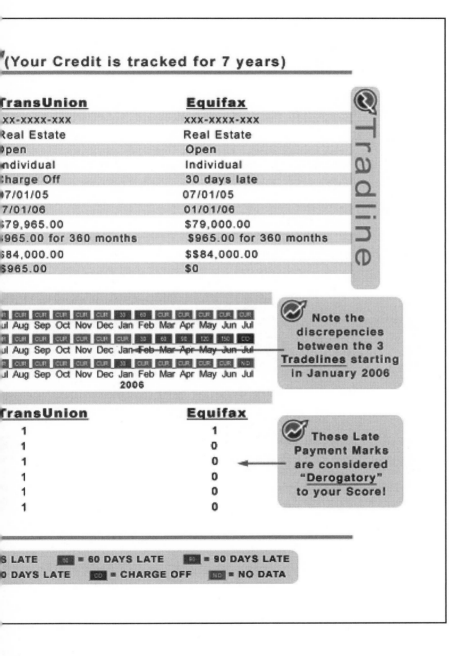

(Your Credit is tracked for 7 years)

TransUnion	Equifax
XX-XXXX-XXX	XXX-XXXX-XXX
Real Estate	Real Estate
Open	Open
Individual	Individual
Charge Off	30 days late
07/01/05	07/01/05
7/01/06	01/01/06
$79,965.00	$79,000.00
$965.00 for 360 months	$965.00 for 360 months
$84,000.00	$$84,000.00
$965.00	$0

Jul Aug Sep Oct Nov Dec Jan Feb Mar Apr May Jun Jul
Jul Aug Sep Oct Nov Dec Jan Feb Mar Apr May Jun Jul
Jul Aug Sep Oct Nov Dec Jan Feb Mar Apr May Jun Jul
2006

Note the discrepencies between the 3 Tradelines starting in January 2006

TransUnion	Equifax
1	1
1	0
1	0
1	0
1	0
1	0

These Late Payment Marks are considered "Derogatory" to your Score!

S LATE   = 60 DAYS LATE   = 90 DAYS LATE
0 DAYS LATE   = CHARGE OFF   = NO DATA

are not self-explanatory and are referred to as "Positive," "Negative," or "Non-rated." A summary rating of "Positive" indicates that you are the kind of person who pays on time, a "Negative" shows severe credit problems, and a "Non-rated is an indication of a new account. Of course, negative entries on your credit report reflect poorly on your credit score. **Your goal should be to dispute and eventually have removed all inaccurate and negative items that appear in your credit report.**

The Account-History-Information Section of your credit report includes the names of all agencies that have extended credit to you. It states the account number, describes the account type, includes the account's condition, states whether the account is individual or joint, and tells whether it is open or closed. It also gives the date you opened it and the date you closed it.

The Account-History-Information Section shows the balance between the amount you presently owe on the account and your credit limit. This balance is one of the most important pieces of information for future creditors and is the reason you should attempt to keep your monthly balance below 30 percent of your credit limit. Your monthly payment requirements are listed as well as the highest balance that you have ever owed on the account. So are the first time you ever thought about running away from home or kissed your boyfriend or girlfriend. Just kidding about that, but it almost seems like they'd know that, too, doesn't it? Anyway, the credit-reporting agencies keep track of how often you've made late payments and the amount of those payments. Any consumer statements or remarks written by you also appear here.

Some credit reports also include a graph of your payment history over the past two years. Others post a graph describing a four-year payment history. Yet another graph (usually found at the bottom of the report) may contain a seven-year history, with special attention given to any late payments you may have made.

Public-Record-Information Section

This section lists information about legal matters affecting your credit that is available to the general public. Negative entries may also appear in the Public-Record-Information Section. You should examine this area for accuracy as well. Examples of negative items include bankruptcies, tax liens, court judgments, and unpaid child-support payments.

For each public record, some or all of the following terms and information may appear on your credit report. Some of these may seem self-explanatory, but occasionally a term will appear that isn't what you might think. Please forgive me if some of these are obvious, but it never hurts to be certain when it comes to deciphering credit reports.

Type: This simply refers to the type of record. Some examples are tax liens, bankruptcies, and judgments.

Status: This refers to the record's current status.

5 # Public Record Infor

Bankruptcy

Experi

Type:	Chapter
Status:	Filed
Date File-Reported:	08/06/03
How Filed:	Ind Acct
Reference #:	2A-123-4
Closing Date:	10/14/03
Court:	Local Co
Liability:	$65,000.
Exempt Amount:	$1500.00
Asset Amount:	$20,000.
Remarks:	

The Public Record Section lists pubicly available info that may affect your "Credit Worthiness". These might include Civil Actions, Bankruptcy, Tax Leins and more.

6 # Inquiry Information

Creditor Name	Inqui
ACME BANK	04/23/
USA Credit Card Corp	11/15/
USA Credit Card Corp	12/01/
Local Merchant	09/03/
Local Auto Lender	02/11/

Inquiries to your Credit Report may be originated by many different sources. Too many inquiries can negatively affect your Score!

7 # Creditor Informatio

Creditor Name	Addr
ACME BANK	3030
ACME Mortgage	2020
USA Credit Card Corp.	2000
Local Auto Lender	222 C
Local Merchant	102 S

The Creditor Info Section lists the names of current and potential creditors that appear on your Credit Report including History and Inquiries.

Bankruptcy stays on your Report for 10 years!

TransUnion	Equifax
Chapter 7 Bankruptcy	Chapter 7 Bankruptcy
Filed	Filed
08/06/03	08/06/03
Individual Acct	Individual Account
2A-123-456	2A-123-456
10/14/03	10/14/03
Local Court	Local Court
$65,000.00	$65,000.00
$1500.00	$1500.00
$20,000.00	$20,000.00

s on your Credit Report for 2 years

Credit Bureau
TransUnion
Experian
Equifax
TransUnion
Experian

ys on your Credit Report for 2-7 years

	Phone Number
rtown, CO 80000	800-111-1111
rcity, CO 80010	800-111-2222
, NY 10010	800-111-3333
rcity, CO 80010	800-111-4444
rtown, CO 80000	800-111-5555

Date Filed/Reported: This is the date of the initial filing of the record.

How Filed: This is the your role in filing the record. In
most cases, the record is filed individually or jointly.

Reference Number: Each record has its own identifying number.

Closing/Released Date: This is either the date that
the record was closed or the date that the judgment
was awarded.

Court: This refers to the court or agency with jurisdic-
tion over the record.

Amount: This is the amount of the judgment or lien
stated in U.S. dollars.

Remarks: If any remarks made by you or the court appear in the Public-Record-Information Section, they will
be displayed here.

**If the public record includes a bankruptcy, three oth-
er fields show up. They are:**

Liability: This is the amount that the bankruptcy court
has required you to pay to creditors.

Exempt Amount: Sometimes the court will find that you are not legally responsible for the total amount the lender is requesting. The amount you do not have to pay is called the exempt amount.

Asset Amount: In a bankruptcy proceeding, the court totals your assets to determine what is available for satisfying the demands of creditors.

The Inquiry-Information Section

This section of your credit report lists inquiries that have been made into your credit history. This information includes the date of the inquiry and the name of the creditor making it. An inquiry appears on your credit report when a potential creditor requests a copy.

Inquiries are accepted only if you have an established credit relationship with the requester or if you are applying for new credit. The name or the entity requesting the information will appear on your credit report, thus permitting you to know and track who is seeking your credit information.

PLEASE NOTE! An excessive number of inquiries may adversely affect your creditworthiness. You should dispute any inaccurate inquiries. If you inquire into your own credit, however, those

> *inquiries do not count against you. Also, inquiries bunched together during a short time period will generally not harm your credit score because the credit-reporting agencies usually assume that you are shopping for a home or automobile loan.*

The Creditor-Information Section

This section shows all creditors that are listed on your credit report. The names of creditors from the Account-History Section and Inquiry Section also appear in this section, along with the creditors' addresses and telephone numbers. You must use regular mail to contact creditors for whom telephone numbers are not listed on the credit report.

Some Creditors Don't Report to the Credit Bureaus

Why? Because credit-reporting agencies charge a fee each time a creditor gives them a piece of information about you, and some creditors don't want to spend the money. While they may check on your credit score before they do business with you, they often don't report back to the credit-reporting agencies. These creditors often include insurance carriers, landlords, hospitals, physicians, tradesmen and tradeswomen, local finance companies, utility companies, and credit unions.

More Credit Jargon

Okay, here are some more initials, abbreviations, and insider terms that some credit-reporting agencies still use. It's important to become familiar with them, because the credit report will appear much less confusing once you understand the terminology. This general information should help you make sense of your credit report.

> **NOT PAY AA**—This term refers to an outstanding balance that exists on the account and indicates that you are not paying according to the credit agreement. You should do your best to avoid this kind of negative entry.

> **CHARGE-OFF or CHARGED TO P & L (profit and loss)**—This means the lender wrote off the debt because it believed the debt to be uncollectable. Just because the debt was written off, however, doesn't mean that it won't weigh in as a negative in your credit-score calculation. In fact, these types of actions are considered to be some of the most damaging to your credit score.

> **30-DAY**—You have made a payment that was at least 30-days late.

> **60-DAY**—This indicates that you made at least one payment 60-days late.

90-DAY—You could be sent to Alcatraz for this one. Just kidding. It means, of course, that you have a payment that was at least 90-days late. You may not spent time on "The Rock" for it, but this will almost certainly lower your credit scores, so try to avoid being this late.

IN Installment Account—This refers to an account with a fixed number of specified payments. Mortgages or automobile loans are common examples.

RV Revolving Account—This type of account employs regular monthly payments. Credit-card accounts function as revolving accounts.

MN Open/Monthly Account—This acronym stands for an account that must be paid in full after each billing. This type of account is not common.

OT/Other Company's Account Being Collected—This is an account of an unknown type that has been turned over to a collection agency.

Unknown Account (UN)—If you are borrowing money from the Godfather, it is most likely a UN, or unknown account. By the way, I strongly suggest not going to the mob for loans. Their terms can be murder. I probably don't need to give you this advice, but it is best not to get into risky loans from unknown lenders. The best advice is to stay traditional and safe.

DEED IN LIEU—This is shorthand for giving a creditor a deed to your property to prevent foreclosure on your home. It also indicates that the mortgage debt you owed is now paid and the account is now current.

GOVCLAIM—This means that Uncle Sam is not happy with you. It indicates you failed to repay a government loan, and the government has filed a claim against you.

FORECLOSURE—The lender seized your property because you failed to pay the mortgage payments.

VOL SURR—This stands for "voluntarily surrendered." Its appearance on your credit report indicates that you have voluntarily surrendered the property in order to prevent repossession by a creditor.

REPO—This tells the story that your property was repossessed because you failed to repay the loan. Someone made a bad movie by this name, but in real life, this isn't a drama in which you should want to play a primary role.

How to Improve Your Credit Score

Once you have received and reviewed your credit report, it's time to take action. Follow the instructions set forth below, and be sure to pay your bills on time! The goal is to delete all dated, incomplete, and damaging information from your credit report, to add accurate information, and to start making a track record of meeting scheduled payments. Faithfully doing this will significantly improve your credit score in just a few months!

Reviewing Your Credit Reports for Errors

Did you know that more than fifty-four *billion* pieces of data are added to credit reports each year? Add that to the fact that credit-reporting agencies do not check the validity of the information they receive (they just plug it into your account profile as they receive it from your creditors), and it is little wonder that errors occur so frequently in credit reports. Each time you access your credit report, be sure to check the information contained in it for accuracy. The most common mistakes are:

- listings of accounts that are not yours,
- accounts that are paid or closed and are reported as carrying a balance, and
- records of late payments that are not true.

Another common error occurs after a bankruptcy. The credit bureaus are often slow to adjust their records, and accounts sometimes show balances owed long after a bankruptcy has been declared. This can be annoying, but such obvious errors will not be eliminated unless you take action. Don't be shy. If I can do it, you certainly can. Here's what you do. Highlight each item you wish to dispute, paying special attention to the name of the creditor and the account number. You will need to input this information into the *Recreditpair* Letter Generator. Remember, you are responsible for determining which accounts need verification!

How to Dispute Credit-File Information and Errors

After reviewing your credit report, use the *Recreditpair* Letter Generator to create your letters to the credit-reporting agencies. With each letter, you should include a copy of your credit report and highlight the items you are disputing. If you are disputing more than one item in your letter, you need to include only one copy of your report. The credit-reporting agency must respond to your complaint within 30 days. If you don't receive a response within that time, send a follow-up letter. Follow-up dispute letters are located in the Letter Generator.

Persistence is the key to success. Often the credit bureau will respond with a letter stating that your dispute is frivolous. Don't allow yourself to be pushed around. Resend your

dispute letter, and include as much supporting documentation as possible. This additional documentation may consist
of cancelled checks, letters from the original creditor, and
any proof of payment. Let the credit bureau know that you
are not going to quit until it fixes the error.

As I mentioned before, I recommend that you dispute no
more than one-third of the inaccurate items on your credit
report within a 30-day period. Disputing all of the inaccurate
items at the same time increases your chances of receiving a
frivolous-dispute letter.

Other Steps Toward Fixing Your Record

As you may already know, thousands of so-called credit-
repair consultants charge their clients to "fix" their credit.
As a matter of fact, though, most of what they do involves
disputing negative items on your credit report in order to
have them removed. You can save money and headaches by
disputing the errors yourself!

FINDING AND CORRECTING MISTAKES—
Although inaccuracies do not deserve a place on any credit
report, it's likely that you'll find at least one and perhaps
more on yours. Let's suppose that an open collection for one
hundred dollars appears on your credit report even though
you paid it two years ago. Disputing the accuracy of the item
with the credit bureaus is simply exercising your right under the Fair Credit Reporting Act to have the item corrected.
The law requires the creditor to verify the disputed item and
respond to the credit bureau within 30 days. If they find that

the item is old or inaccurate, most creditors will inform the credit bureau, and the credit bureau will delete it. You should be prepared, though, to prove to the creditor that the item is inaccurate, perhaps by showing a canceled check for payment or offering other substantiating information.

ASKING FOR A REINVESTIGATION—At times, credit bureaus delete accurate items from your credit reports, and at other times, they omit positive facts about your credit status. These things happen because the creditor chooses not to reinvestigate and respond to the credit bureau's notification. Remember, the creditor has 30 days to respond once you file a request. If the creditor does not do so, the credit-reporting agencies must remove the negative information from your credit reports. Of course, knowingly disputing accurate information that appears on your credit report is illegal, but if you find inaccurate or incomplete items there, you should take action to get them corrected or removed.

TALK DIRECTLY TO CREDITORS—Remember, you are permitted to talk to your creditors directly. You must be assertive and not hesitate to face them. I recommend being polite, but firm. Ask if they are willing to request that their account be deleted from your credit report. When I was working on improving my credit status, I called my credit-card companies and asked to be put in contact with the internal department that reported my accounts. Once connected to the proper person, I explained my hardship and politely asked that the company remove the negative item from my credit report. Every creditor did so without delay. This is a good strategy because the credit-card companies and the other entities that loan you money are the original creditors who deliver to the credit-reporting agencies the information that appears in your credit report. The credit-reporting agencies simply report what the creditors tell them to report. Going to the source is frequently the best method. Every negative item removed from your credit report is another step toward your overall goal of improving your credit score.

If the account in dispute is inaccurate, the credit-reporting agency must delete it from your credit report. It bears repeating that if the creditor does not respond within 30 days of being notified of your dispute, the credit-reporting agency must delete the account. Dispute, and be persistent! Believe me, it's worth the effort.

How Long do Items Stay on Your Report?

The quick answer is a long time. For example, accurate negative information can stay on your report for seven years, and some items remain even longer. It isn't hard to guess who convinced Congress to make these laws. The creditors did everything they could to severely punish those who do not pay their loans on time—even when the fault consists of a single late payment. Late payments can stay on your credit report and cause you trouble for years, although a single late payment usually won't cause too much mischief. Still, items like bankruptcy can remain on your record for up to ten years! For whatever reason, information reported because of an application for employment with a salary of more than $20,000 has no time limitation. Information reported because of an application for life insurance also has no time limitation.

Lawsuits or judgments against you can remain on your credit report for seven years or until the statute of limitations runs, whichever is longer. Default information concerning U.S.-government-insured loans or U.S-government-guaranteed student loans can stay on your credit report for seven years after certain legal actions. Tax liens appear on the report for seven years after the date of payment.

"Soft-hit inquiries" into your credit stay on your credit report only about six months; however, "hard-hit inquiries" can remain on your profile for up to two years.

How to Use the *Recreditpair* Letter Generator

After reviewing your credit report and highlighting the items you feel are inaccurate, it's time to move to the next step in the *Recreditpair* process. The *Recreditpair* software system is designed to make this important step quick and easy. Here are the steps you should take:

1) Open the *Recreditpair* software program and select "Generate" from the Main Menu.

2) Complete the required fields in the personal-information section of the Letter Generator. The Letter Generator will automatically include this information in the appropriate places in all letters you create with the system.

3) Select the credit-reporting agency to which you intend to send the dispute letter. *Recreditpair* makes letter drafting easy. Since questionable items may appear on any or all of your credit reports, you must send separate letters to each credit-reporting agency. Simply check the box next to the name of the credit-reporting agency you wish to contact, and *Recreditpair* will format the letter automatically. If you check more than one credit-reporting agency, *Recreditpair* will format a separate letter for each one. *Recreditpair* will also automatically print an additional copy of each letter for your file. Keeping good records is of paramount importance when you are working to improve your credit.

4) Choose the letter that best fits your needs. For example, if you are disputing a late payment that appears on your credit report for the first time, select the Dispute letter. If you cannot find a letter that matches your specific problem, use the Custom Letter to create your own personalized dispute letter. All of the letters in the Letter Generator are examples, however, so you can alter any of them to fit your specific situation.

5) After you have completed your letter, click on "print." You need not fill in the personal information (name, address, telephone, and social-security number) or the specific credit-bureau information, because *Recreditpair* does it for you! *Recreditpair* automatically prints four copies of each letter—one for each of the three credit-reporting agencies and one for your file. Be sure to read the printed letter carefully to ensure that it clearly states your complaint.

6) The final step is to prepare your envelopes for mailing. You can find the mailing addresses in the printed letters and in Part II of this book. Follow the mailing instructions at the end of this chapter.

Common Reasons to File a Dispute

Problem	Resolution
My personal information is inaccurate	Provide both the incorrect and corrected information. Include the creditor's name, account number, and reason why the account should be removed from your credit report. Reasons can be things like: the account belongs to another person, the account is outdated, etc.
The following account does not belong on my credit report:	Include the creditor's name, the account number, a description of what is wrong, and how the problem should be corrected.
The following account has inaccurate balance information and needs to be corrected:	This information is inaccurate. The debt was paid on (fill in date). Include the creditor's name, account number, and supporting documentation, such as copies of receipts, canceled checks, letters from the creditor, and so forth.
The following account was reported as being 30-days late:	State that you paid the account in full. Include the creditor's name, account number, and supporting documentation, such as copies of receipts, canceled checks, and letters from the creditor.

Problem	Resolution
The following account was reported as derogatory, which is inaccurate:	Include the creditor's name, the account number, a description of what is wrong, and how the problem should be corrected.
The following account is described erroneously and needs to be corrected:	Include the creditor's name, the account number, and any evidence of closure.
The following account was closed at my request, but is not listed accurately on my report:	Include the creditor's name, date of inquiry, and the reasons that the inquiry should be removed from you credit report.
The following inquiry does not belong on my credit report:	Reasons can be things like: the inquiry is more than two-years old; the inquiry was unauthorized, and so forth.

Keeping track of all correspondence with the credit-reporting agencies, creditors, and debt collectors is extremely important. You should save copies of all documents and correspondence, and you should make a written log of all telephone conversations, making careful note of the date, time, and substance of each conversation you engage in about your accounts and your credit report. The *Recreditpair* software automatically prints file copies of all letters. If you diligently follow the *Recreditpair* process, and the credit bureaus violate the law, you will have the necessary documentation to prove it. You should maintain files of all your records for at least five years, in case something reappears on your report and you need to request that the credit-reporting agencies remove the item again.

Mailing Instructions

As you proceed through these steps, keep copies and records of all correspondence that you send and receive. This includes copies of letters, bills, e-mail messages, faxes, and even the envelopes you send (to provide additional proof of mailing and the date).

I recommend sending all correspondence by Certified Mail with a Return Receipt, so you have written proof of mailing. Using Certified Mail gives you a receipt stamped with the date of mailing and an item number that you can use online to verify the delivery. With the Return Receipt, you should elect the regular-mail option so that you'll receive a green postcard in the mail with the recipient's signature indicating receipt of the letter. The U.S. Postal Service offers a variety of mailing options, proof-of-mailing options, tracking options, and proof-of-delivery options, so before sending each letter, you should think through what kind of proof of mailing and proof of receipt of delivery you want and then discuss it with the postal employee before mailing the letter. Online options exist for tracking, but you should select a means of mailing that provides you with physical proof of both the mailing and the receipt of your letter. You can find detailed information about mailing, proof, and tracking at the USPS website: www.usps.com.

Here are some procedures to follow when corresponding with creditors, debt collectors, or credit-reporting agencies:

1. Write and customize your letter using the *Recreditpair* Letter Generator, then print it.

2. The Letter Generator will automatically print letters addressed to each of the three major credit bureaus and an extra copy for your file. With the letter, you must include proof of your Social Security Number and your current address. You can send either a copy of your Social Security Card, a pay stub or W-2 Form that includes your name and Social Security Number. For proof of address, you may include a copy of your driver's license, or a rental agreement, pay stub or utility bill that includes your name and address. Make cer-

tain you send in photocopies! Do not send originals as you may never see them again.

3. Sign the letter and write the date beside your signature.

4. Make copies of the envelope and any attachments for your file.

5. Staple the originals of the attachments to the Letter-Generator file copy of your letter and file them. You should keep them in a safe place for at least five years.

6. Insert your original letter and copies of the attachments into the envelope and make certain you have properly addressed the envelope to the company to which the letter is addressed. If you do not have the company's mailing address, try searching the Internet or calling the company to confirm the address.

7. Send the letter by Certified Mail with a Return Receipt. (Please see the introductory paragraphs to this subsection for a more complete explanation of the mailing options.) Ask the postal employee to provide you with a receipt for the postage, and be sure you don't leave without some form of postal document that proves the mailing. For each set of letters you send, make sure you have the following in your file:

- A copy of your signed letter;
- Your original attachments;
- A date-stamped cash receipt from the post office;
- A certificate of mailing or other postal document proving mailing, and
- A Return Receipt signed by a representative of the company you have contacted.

I suggest that you save your documents in a file folder or a large envelope marked with the date and name of the company you are contacting. This initial letter will probably lead to further correspondence, and you'll want to keep the information in one place. If you do any of your communication via e-mail, be sure to print a copy of the e-mail message and file it.

These precautions may seem like a hassle, but the pay-offs can be huge. Frequently, if errors have occurred, you will obtain the remedy you seek. With persistence, you can get your records corrected and continue your life with the financial future and good credit you deserve.

PART IV

PART IV

How to Negotiate With Collection Agencies

Almost everyone does it, sooner or later. You forget to make a payment on a debt or run into rough financial times and fail to pay a bill. As we all know, after 180 days of not being paid, the delinquent account often ends up in the typically aggressive hands of a collection agency. Much as a shark "owns" its prey, the collection agency now "owns" your debt. You may be surprised to learn that when your debt is passed to a collection agency, you owe the money to the collection agency and not to the original creditor. You must deal directly with them, which is not always an enjoyable experience.

Before dealing with a collection agency, you should be aware that the agency makes nothing unless you pay some or all of the debt. This may sound ominous, but it can operate in your favor. If you are willing to work with them, collection agencies are sometimes willing to reduce the amount you owe. Some will even set up payment plans and refrain from reporting the collection to the credit bureaus. Others won't budge, though, and will force you to pay the entire debt.

You should know, however, that cutting a deal for reduced payment with a collection agency is vastly different from a "charge-off," which is where the creditor writes off your unpaid debt as a loss. Many people make the mistake of thinking that when creditors charge off their bad debts, they are in the clear. Not by a long shot. **In fact, a charge-off is one of the worst things that can appear on your credit report, especially if it remains unpaid for an extended period of time.** It can even lurk in the darkness for a while, only to be resurrected by a bottom-feeding collection company that decides to take the case to court. Just when you think the issue is dead, it suddenly emerges to make your life difficult. Many debtors have been forced to pay through wage garnishments, with legal expenses added to the judgment. If you can possibly avoid it, do not allow your collection debt to become a charge-off.

Stop Debt Collectors Who Threaten You

The behavior of collection agencies is controlled by federal guidelines set forth in The Fair Debt Collection Practices Act (FDCPA), although it may not seem like it when you receive harassing telephone calls and letters. If a collection agency is pummeling you, you might want to inform yourself of your rights at the Federal Trade Commission website: www.ftc.gov. Remember, debt collectors are able to settle for less than the full amount.

Debt collectors are **not** allowed to:

- Use threats
- Harass you
- Deceive you
- Lie about consequences

When You've been Notified of a Collection Action

I want to help prepare you in the event that a collection agency notifies you of a collection action, but first you should know that two different types of collections exist. The first is a "fresh collection," which means that you have received your first notice on that specific delinquent debt. This notification usually consists of an introductory letter informing you that the account has been turned over to a third party for collection. It also usually states that you have ten days to dispute its accuracy in writing. **If you do not respond, the collection agency will assume the debt is valid and will soon demand payment.** The good news is that you may receive many letters of this nature before the debt becomes a collection reported on your credit report. You should take immediate action, however, in order to avoid its appearance there.

The second type of collection is one that already appears on your credit report. You may not have known of the collection until you received your report. This can occur for many reasons. Perhaps you moved and your mail was not forwarded, or maybe you purposely refused to pay the bill while trying to resolve a misunderstanding with the creditor. Another possibility is that you put a questionable bill aside to evaluate it later and then you forgot about it. (With respect to this last example, I'm speaking from personal experience.) Whatever the reason, you should address the issues head-on, and if any inaccuracies are working against you, dispute them with a letter.

Let's discuss the first type of collection. **If you receive a notice of collection from a collection agency, and you believe you do not owe any money, you must first dispute the collection directly with the collection agency**. The best approach is to simply tell them why the debt is invalid. I once received a collection notice for a delinquent medical payment. I had medical insurance at the time the alleged event occurred, and the insurance company ultimately paid the bill that was in dispute. I wrote a letter to the collection agency informing them of the inaccuracy and refused to pay the bill. Even though I sent follow-up letters, I heard nothing further from them. After carefully checking my credit report for the next few years, however, I verified that no negative information regarding the bill appeared on my credit report. Expecting a collection agency to respond to your correspondence is reasonable, but they don't always do so.

Even if the debt is valid, however, everyone in the game has an opportunity to win. As I stated earlier, collection agencies only make money if they collect some or all of the debt. This is where your negotiating skills come into play. Don't worry if you aren't an experienced negotiator. Negotiation is not so difficult as you may think. A suggested plan of action follows:

Identify Your Goals:

You should clarify in your mind what you want to accomplish. This should include convincing the collection agency to waive any extra fees, reduce the amount you owe, refrain from contacting your credit bureaus, and set up a payment plan. You may not be able to achieve all four of these goals, but you should expect to reach most of them.

Send a Letter to the Collection Agency

Once you have identified your goals, your next step is to use the Letter Generator to draft a letter to send to the collection agency. You should resist negotiating with numbers at first. In fact, do not offer any numbers at all, because the first rule of negotiation is: **WHOEVER SPEAKS FIRST LOSES!** You should wait for the creditor to make the initial settlement offer. You can then counter-offer with a lower amount. If you offer a settlement amount first and the collection agency accepts it, you'll never know if you offered more money than necessary.

Remember, negotiation is an effort by two sides to reach an agreement. Don't go into it thinking you want to beat the collection agency. You are trying to reach a compromise, to find a payoff amount that is satisfactory to both of you. Ask the collection representative to state the lowest amount the collection agency will accept to settle the debt. The answer will give you a starting point for the remainder of the negotiation. Collection representatives always ask for more money than they are authorized to accept. Their job is to maximize the amount paid on the debt. You should counter-offer with a figure of your own and then work toward agreeing on an amount that you can comfortably pay. If the person you're talking with is rude or does not seem interested in negotiating, don't get angry. Thank the representative for the assistance and calmly ask to speak to a supervisor. Once you get the supervisor on the line, start over with your negotiation. Sometimes, supervisors won't budge either, but most collection agencies will eventually deal with you.

When you reach an agreement, be sure to get it in writing before you pay anything on the debt. Also, part of the deal must include the collection agency's agreement not to report the collection to the credit-reporting agencies. This must also be in writing.

Be prepared to pay if you make a deal! If you offer a lump sum, the collection agency will probably give you a bigger discount than if you suggest payment arrangements.

Now let's talk about collections that already appear on your record. If you believe that a collection that is listed on your credit report is not valid, you should dispute it. Use the *Recreditpair* Letter Generator to draft the letter, and be sure to customize it to your specific situation. The collection is probably on the records of all three credit-reporting agencies, so you should contact them all. As with other inaccuracies you find on your reports, the credit-reporting agencies must remove them if they are unverified or if the creditor does not confirm the legitimacy of the debt.

If the collection is valid, it's time to call the collection agency. You will find the telephone number on the credit report. The process of dealing with the collection agency is the same as in the first example. The only difference is that the agreement should include a provision that the collection agency report the collection to the credit-reporting agencies as paid. Again, get the agreement in writing. A paid collection is much better than an unpaid one. It shows lenders that you are honest and willing to make right your credit situation. This will go a long way at the time of making your next major purchase.

Be prepared to face the stubborn collection agency or creditor that demands that you provide proof of your inability to pay. This can cause delays, and you may need to work with a nonprofit credit-counseling agency or an attorney in order to get the issue resolved. It's important to realize, however, that you can do much of this yourself. Try everything you can to convince your creditors to work with you, but if you cannot convince them creditor to budge, find an expert to help you. Be sure to act quickly, because ignoring your debts is the worst thing you can do. It might take some hard work on your part, but you'll feel great when you finally get the issues resolved.

PART V

PART V

How to Avoid Having Your Identity Stolen

Identity theft can have a devastating effect on your credit. The Federal Trade Commission (FTC) recently reported that this is one of the fastest-growing crimes in the nation. It is terribly intrusive and can seriously disrupt your ability to lead a normal life. Here are some of the ways thieves can gather enough information to steal your identity, according to the FTC:

- They may steal your mail, including your financial correspondence.

- They may obtain information from documents in your trash or recycling bin. This is a common method of pilfering your private information. Purchasing and using a shredder is an excellent way to avoid this problem.

- They may use the Internet to hack into your computer files or those of an online retailer with which you have done business, or they may run Internet scams whereby, through some type of ruse, they request your credit-card number and perhaps your social-security number. You should never provide such information over the Internet or to an unverified telephone solicitor.

- They may bribe employees who work with private information.

- They may obtain your account numbers and other information by stealing your purse or wallet.

- They may use a change-of-address form to have your mail forwarded to a location of their choosing.

Other sneaky methods exist, as well, but you get the idea. Identity thieves use this information to charge any number of things to you, from office supplies and groceries to luxury automobiles and cruises. They may take out an automobile loan or establish a wireless telephone service in your name (a favorite trick of drug smugglers who use the telephone to set up contacts), and they may open a bank account using your name and write bad checks on it. They sometimes open dozens of credit-card accounts using the identities of others and charge thousands of dollars on them. Wouldn't you be surprised to find you have several-hundred-thousand dollars of credit-card bills and bad checks?

Here are some tips to keep your information safe:

1) Shred all old credit-card statements, bills, correspondence, credit-card offers, and any other documents that contain personal information.

2) Never leave credit-card receipts or debit-card receipts at a bank, ATM, or store. Take them with you, and shred them at home.

3) Mail envelopes containing payment for bills at a public mailbox or at the post office. Don't put them in your home mailbox, because it is too vulnerable to theft.

4) Keep your birth certificate, social-security card, and passport locked away securely, so they can't be stolen.

5) Change your bank passwords and PIN numbers frequently, and never use birth dates, anniversary dates, children's names, or pets' names that can be guessed easily.

6) Never keep your PIN numbers filed in your computer if you use that computer to access the Internet.

Hackers can access everything in your computer with relative ease.

7) Be wary of offers from unknown solicitors or companies. The bad guys know how to create fraudulent, official-looking credit applications. These schemes offer you pre-approved credit if you provide your mother's maiden name, social-security number, address, income, etc.

8) Be wary of requests to update your personal information that appear to come from companies with which you normally do business. Any request to update your personal information, whether by telephone or over the Internet should raise a red flag. Legitimate businesses seldom contact customers in this way for this purpose. Do not provide the information! Call the company directly via a known telephone number and ask for a verification of the request. If the contact proves fraudulent, the company may ask your assistance in supplying information to identify the source. All legitimate companies and the federal government take such criminal activity seriously.

9) You may have heard of "phishing." Phishing is computer-hackers' jargon that refers to e-mail or pop-up messages that trick you into thinking you are dealing with a legitimate company. Crooks who use this

technique will first ask you to verify your personal information and then to verify your user name and password. Many of these messages and websites look legitimate. If you suspect that an e-mail message or other communication is fraudulent, do not reply to it. Most Internet merchants and financial institutions have security teams that may ask you to forward the full message or hyperlink to help them investigate the questionable site.

10) Never use e-mail to send important personal or financial information. Most e-mail accounts are not secure!

11) Hold onto your purse or wallet!

You can find practical tips from the federal government and the technology industry to help you guard against phishing and Internet fraud at www.onguardonline.gov.

PART VI

PART VI

What to Do if Your Identity is Stolen

According to the Federal Trade Commission website, identity theft occurs when someone, without your authorization, uses your name, social-security number, date of birth, or other identifying information to commit fraud. For example, someone may commit identity theft by using your personal information to open a credit-card account or obtain a loan in your name.

For more information, visit www.consumer.com.gov/idtheft, or write to: Federal Trade Commission, Consumer Response Center, Room 130-B, 600 Pennsylvania Avenue, N.W. Washington, D.C., 20580.

The Fair Credit Reporting Act (FRCA) gives you specific rights when you believe that you are the victim of identity theft. Here is a brief summary of the rights designed to help you recover from identity theft. Most of this information can be found on the FTC website under Consumer Protection / ID Theft Privacy & Security / Identity Theft / Take Charge: Fighting Back Against Identity Theft.

If you believe you are a victim of identity fraud, you should place a fraud alert on your credit reports. The three credit-reporting agencies have toll-free numbers for reporting fraud. You only need to call one of them, and that agency must, under the law, contact the other two.

The three fraud-alert telephone numbers are:

Equifax: 1-800-525-6285
Experian: 1-888-397-3742
TransUnion: 1-800-680-7289

You should also order a free copy of your credit report. Review it carefully, and, according to the FTC, "look for inquiries from companies you haven't contacted, accounts you did not open, and debts on your accounts that you cannot explain." If you see anything you do not recognize, have it taken off your credit report immediately.

Two Types of Fraud Alert

The FTC website discusses two types of fraud alert. The first is an "initial alert" that stays on your credit report for at least 90 days. This is the type of alert you should request if you suspect you've been ripped off by an identity thief. The second is an "extended alert" that comes into play after you've become a known victim of identity theft. It stays on your credit report for seven years. This alert is initiated after you've provided the credit-reporting agency with an identity-theft report stating that you are an identity-theft victim. The credit-reporting agencies will remove your name from marketing lists for prescreened-credit offers for five years unless you request that the ban be lifted. Both types of fraud alert require appropriate documentation from you verifying that the identity theft occurred. The fraud alerts cause delays in processing loan applications and may cause other slowdowns as well, but they help protect you at the same time.

The documentation will include a police report outlining the theft and any losses you've incurred. You should also file a complaint with the Federal Trade Commission at www.consumer.gov/idtheft or at their toll-free line: 1-877-IDTHEFT (1-887-438-4338).

THE FEDERAL TRADE COMMISSION WEBSITE

If you think you may be an identity-theft victim, or you simply want to protect yourself against the possibility, I highly recommend you peruse the Federal Trade Commission website. It provides tips for protecting yourself, and it gives contact information for all of the entities with which you should communicate. It also contains:

- A number of tips for organizing your case to resolve identity theft;
- How to deal with fraudulent checks;
- How to deal with fraudulent accounts opened in your name;
- Where to find help;
- Instruction for fighting bankruptcy fraud;
- Instructions for correcting fraudulent information on your credit reports;
- Detailed tips for preventing identity theft, and
- What the law says about identity theft.

The website also shows how to protect your Social Security Number and gives a bibliography of books and pamphlets that contain information pertaining to identity theft. It's worth browsing the site, even if you've never thought about identity theft and have no reason to believe that anyone is tampering with your information. Doing so may prompt you to take precautions that could save you from the massive headaches that identity theft can cause you.

PART VII

PART VII

The 25 Biggest Mistakes You Can Make With Your Credit

Mistake 1: Wasting Money on So-Called Credit-Repair Companies or Attorneys

Recreditpair will teach you how to work to improve your credit. You can easily do everything the credit-repair companies do. Once you become knowledgeable about the credit-verification process, you can use *Recreditpair* to help your friends and family check their credit status and correct any discrepancies. Using credit-repair companies is expensive and risky, and if they act outside of the law (a few have been known to do so), you could be held responsible.

Mistake 2: Not Disputing and Correcting Inaccuracies on Your Credit Reports

The appearance of negative or erroneous information on your credit reports can cost you money by driving down your credit scores. The dispute process outlined in this book will assist you in removing damaging information from your credit reports. My advice is to get serious, get moving, and get rid of errors that are creating holes in your pocketbook.

Mistake 3: Not Understanding Your Credit Reports

As you know, your credit report contains vital information. The hieroglyphics that the credit-reporting agencies use in it can be a bit intimidating, at first, so take your time and use the lists of terms provided in this book. Soon you will be on your way to being a credit expert. Anyone can do it, so stay with it, and don't give up.

You need to know your credit scores from each of the three major credit-reporting agencies. Each agency uses a different formula to arrive at its score, and the score variations can be significant. Even though most creditors, such as mortgage companies, base their loan decisions on your mid-score, one low score can drag your credit score downward.

You should set a goal of attaining the highest possible score on all three credit-bureau reports.

Mistake 4: Continually Making Late Payments

You must get into the habit of paying your bills on time. If you remain delinquent on current bills, removing inaccurate information from your credit report will have little effect on your overall credit situation. If you are unable to make your bills current, you may want to consider talking with a consumer-credit-counseling service. The counselor will help you find ways to stop the negative reporting and put you on a faster track to financial stability. Obtaining new accounts during your repayment period is difficult. That may not be such a bad thing, however, because cleaning up the past can take time. Consistently paying your bills on or before their due dates will dramatically change your credit profile.

Mistake 5: Renting Rather Than Owning

Homeownership is a dream that most of us have in common, and the use of *Recreditpair* can make realizing that dream possible. Some people who rent could purchase a home right now, but they don't know it. Surprisingly, many people don't know that it's free to see if they qualify for a home loan. Real-estate loans show stability and can help you obtain higher credit scores. Remember; even if you're denied a home loan, the mortgage broker will help you plan a strategy to eventually realize your dream of homeownership.

Mistake 6: Having Too Many Credit Inquiries on Your Credit Report

Each time someone inquires into your credit status, the inquiry is recorded on your credit reports. Too many inquiries can lower your credit score, because you seem like a high risk to lenders. Credit inquiries that are not initiated by you have no effect on your credit score and are called "soft inquiries." An example of a soft inquiry is a credit inquiry generated by a pre-approved card offer sent to you as an enticement through the mail. If you are shopping for a loan, try to bunch all of your credit inquiries into a two-week period. That way the credit-reporting agencies will recognize what you were doing and, hopefully, consider all inquiries grouped into a small timeframe collectively as a single hit.

Mistake 7: Pursuing too Many "Pre-approved" Credit Offers

The only way to know if you are actually pre-approved is to read the credit application carefully. If it asks for your social-security number, it's likely that you're only pre-qualified. This distinction is important because being pre-qualified simply means the credit-card issuer made a soft inquiry to determine if it might approve your application. If you fill out a credit application that requires your social-security number, more than likely you will create a hard-hit inquiry that could reduce your credit score.

Mistake 8: Choosing the Wrong Credit Card

When I started my credit-recovery process some years ago, few options for credit existed. This is no longer the case. You should avoid applying for credit cards that have high annual fees, high processing fees, and high interest rates. I have seen some credit-card offers that have so many fees attached that by the time the card is approved, you owe almost as much as the card's limit allows! Be smart about your credit-card choices, and you can save significant sums.

Mistake 9: Living Without Major Credit Cards

While it may seem prudent to cut up your credit cards and live without them, this is not a good idea. Lenders will consider you to be a higher risk if you have no major credit cards. Try to stick with the top credit-card companies, such as Visa, MasterCard, Discover, and American Express. It's fine to obtain credit cards through banks or credit unions, but you should confirm that they report to all three credit bureaus.

Mistake 10: Check and Debit Cards are Not Credit

Even though you see the company's logo on your check card, it is not a credit card. Therefore, activity on it is not reported to the major credit-reporting agencies. The use of these cards, although convenient, will not raise your credit scores. You should be aware, however, that misusing these cards can cause collections that negatively affect your scores.

Mistake 11: Not Being Prepared

When you have perfect credit, lenders need little documentation. When you are rebuilding your credit and at the same time seeking a loan, however, you need to be prepared to convince the creditors that you are a good risk. Be ready to produce documentation required for the loan you seek. This varies with each scenario. Generally, though, you should arrive at the loan office with such things as pay stubs, utility bills, references, and copies of tax statements (usually for the past three years). When you come unprepared, the rip-off artists will appear, fangs bared. Some salespeople and loan officers think of unprepared customers as easy targets who can be talked into buying anything at any price. When you are prepared, your chances of being treated with respect increase significantly.

Let me give an example. You walk into a bank for a loan, and the loan officer says, "I need your current pay stub, a full work history including telephone numbers, and a utility bill, or I can't help you." If you don't have this information with you, the sales process has begun by your being told what to do. In the vernacular, this is called "taking control of the customer." You can prevent this by smiling sweetly and responding, "I'm well aware of what I need, and I have it all with me." As a result of your preparation and demeanor, the salesperson is likely to straighten up and treat you with respect. All salespeople are aware that you can take your business to the competition.

Mistake 12: Not Shopping Around

Recreditpair teaches you how to obtain and understand your credit reports. With this knowledge, you can shop for the best deals without accessing your credit reports. If a salesperson claims to need your credit report to determine your interest rate, simply ask for the total payment under a range of interest rates. Most shoppers tend to purchase from the first company that grants loan approval. Remember, you are likely to be approved at many places. A good purchase involves much more than simply being approved for credit. You must work to obtain the best prices and interest rates, as well.

Mistake 13: Not Using Major Banks or Institutions When Borrowing

When you start rebuilding your credit, more often than not, you will have to use finance companies. As a rule, you differentiate among mainstream banks, credit unions, and finance companies by their names. Bob's Bank means it's a bank. Dental-Floss-Federal Credit Union means it's a credit union with great teeth. Acme Finance is obviously a finance company. Having a bank or credit union as a lender helps your credit scores. If you do not qualify for credit at bank or credit union, don't fret. You may want to utilize a finance company while you use *Recreditpair* to strengthen your credit status. If you follow the *Recreditpair* suggestions, your scores will improve enough over time to refinance most loans with better lenders.

Mistake 14: Closing Old Accounts

The length of time you have reported credit improves your credit scores. Closing accounts that have a positive credit history, even if they are not being used, erases that history.

Mistake 15: Making Minimum Credit-Card Payments

Have you ever made a payment and received a subsequent statement showing you owed more than before? This is what

I call credit-card-company math. If you make the minimum payment on some credit cards, it could take you as much as 27 years to pay off the balance. TWENTY-SEVEN YEARS!!! Doubling or tripling the minimum payment will drastically reduce your balance and shorten the payoff to a reasonable time.

Mistake 16: Leaving Your Revolving Credit Balances at or Near the Limit

Your available balances also contribute to the determination of your credit scores. The balance is the remaining credit you have available on an account. For instance, if you have a $1,000 limit on a credit card, and you owe $900 on it, only one-tenth of the card's limit is available to you. You should strive for availability of at least 70 percent of the limit. Consistently running up credit-card bills without paying them down substantially will lower your credit scores. You should strive to pay off your credit cards every month. If that is not possible, keep the balances as low as possible. For a credit card with a $1,000 limit, you should maintain a monthly balance of less than $300.

Mistake 17: Not Using Your Credit

High credit scores are the result of good behavior in the eyes of the credit-reporting agencies. Using your credit and paying on time should be your goal. Don't let credit accounts remain dormant. Make small purchases and pay them off. Remember, paying your accounts off each month will help you obtain the highest possible credit score. Unused accounts can disappear from your credit reports and erase positive credit history.

Mistake 18: Too Much of One Type of Credit

Nutritionists tell us that we should eat balanced meals that contain portions from all food groups. To have healthy credit scores, you also need to achieve balance. If you have nothing but retail credit cards on your report, your score will be lower than if you have a mix of installment, major-revolving, and retail-revolving credit.

Mistake 19: Ignoring Collection Companies

If you have a lingering problem with a collection agency, take action. If you don't believe the amount they say you owe is accurate, dispute it. *Recreditpair* gives you all the tools necessary to accomplish this. If the collection is legitimate, don't pay it until you call the collection company and try to reduce the amount and ask to have it removed from your credit report. You should obtain a written agreement from the collection company that reflects the settlement amount and the collection agency's commitment to remove the item from your credit report.

Mistake 20: Always Paying with Cash

Credit is the ability to acquire debt. While most of us were taught growing up that we should avoid incurring debt, we must rethink that preconception if we want to live in today's world. Accruing debt and paying it off promptly is the new lesson we must learn. Building a credit file by using nothing but cash is impossible. If you hope to own a home, it will probably be difficult to save up the cash to pay for it. Credit, not cash, is king, and we must change our mindset to benefit ourselves.

Mistake 21: Borrowing from Lenders That do not Report to Credit Bureaus

The best example I can give you of a lender that does not report to the credit bureaus is a direct dealer-financed car purchase. Dealers who extend their own credit run what are sometimes referred to as "buy-here-pay-here lots." As a rule, these companies do not report to the three credit bureaus. Since your purchase is not recorded on your credit report, you're stuck buying from the same dealer again on your next purchase. Make certain that your lenders report directly to all three credit bureaus.

Mistake 22: Cosigning for Someone You Don't Really Know

This is a delicate subject. I recommend to people who are rebuilding their credit to find cosigners. On the other side of that coin, however, if you are a cosigner, you should know the person for whom you cosign very well before taking that step. I know of a young lady who wanted to help her new boyfriend get a car. She had good credit, and his was lousy. The automobile loan went through, but the relationship did not. Soon the car was repossessed, and her credit was damaged.

You have to use good judgment. If the person you want to help had good credit at one time, and failing health or an unexpected job lay-off caused the credit problems, the risk may be warranted. On the other hand, some people have never paid their bills on time and must learn on their own that good credit matters.

Mistake 23: Not Protecting Your Credit from Identity Theft

Identity theft is one of the fastest-growing crimes in the world. You already may have been affected by this electronic intrusion. *Recreditpair* teaches you how to obtain and read your credit reports. This is the best defense. You will be instantly alerted if someone is messing with your credit.

Mistake 24: Paying Off Installment Accounts Too Quickly

Over the years, I've heard many homemade, credit-improvement ideas. One that makes me smile is the notion of buying something on credit and paying it off immediately. In the past, this was considered a heroic thing to do. Times have changed, however, and today your credit scores can suffer if you do this. Ironically, they will improve if you keep the accounts open for a while. I'm not saying that it's a bad idea to pay debts quickly. I'm saying that as you rebuild your credit, you need to establish a history of on-time payments. Cars are the most common type of installment credit. If you purchase an automobile, I recommend you pay on it for nine to twelve months before paying off the note.

Mistake 25: Not Being Truthful

One of my favorite quotes is: "If you tell the truth long enough, you'll be found out." Don't tell fibs on your credit applications. Tell the truth even if it hurts. If the loan isn't approved, then focus on other issues in your credit-rebuilding process. You can't fool the banks, so don't bother to try. Every time something about you checks out as true, the lender will be closer to approving your loan.

PART VIII

The 25 Best-Kept Secrets of Credit-Repair Companies

1.) Adding a Trade Line to Your Credit Report.

Adding a trade line to your credit report is the best way to immediately affect your credit score in a positive way. A trade line is an account that is reported on your credit report. Positive trade lines improve your credit scores. If you have poor credit and need help, find a friend, family member, or associate with good credit and ask to add your name to one of that person's credit cards. Doing this makes you an authorized user on the card. Explain that you'll never have to know the account number or take possession of the card. The credit card with your name on it will be sent to the person's home. Ask the person to charge five dollars on the card and then keep it or cut it up. This should be a credit card that has been open for a long time and has a low balance or is paid off entirely every month. Your friend's good credit will help you. (Of course, if the person does not pay bills on time, this will have a negative effect on your credit score, so choose your white knight wisely.) In addition to thanking your friend for helping you, it would be a good idea to pay the five dollars in cash at the time you make the request.

2) Keep Your Balances Below 30 Percent.

Credit bureaus use many variables to calculate your final credit scores. One of the factors considered is your available balance. People who peg their credit-card balances at the maximum limits every month are considered higher risks than those who maintain low balances. For example, if you have a credit card that has a balance of $1,000, you should pay it down at least to $300 each month. Maintaining a balance of less than ten percent of the maximum is even better.

3) All Information on a Trade Line Must Be Accurate.

The dollar amount is not the only thing that must be correct on your credit-bureau reports. Many other items, such as account numbers, opening dates, closing dates, and dates of final payment, must be reflected accurately. If you sincerely believe that any of the information is inaccurate, you should file a dispute. Filing a dispute on accurate information is illegal. At times, however, you may not be able to easily confirm the accuracy of the information, and a dispute may be appropriate.

4) Negotiate with Collection Companies.

You may find collections on your credit reports about which you know nothing. This underscores the importance of monitoring your credit reports. Of course, collection accounts that you know about also appear on the reports. If you discover a collection on your credit report, contact the collection agency and attempt to negotiate a reduced amount or more-favorable payment scheme. Kindly explain that you never intended to have a collection and ask if they will remove the collection from your credit report if you agree to make payment. If they say yes, get it in writing either by fax or mail. If they agree, you need to be prepared to pay.

5) Don't Use Finance Companies.

The type of lender you choose can affect your credit scores. Finance companies traditionally charge higher interest rates than banks or major automobile lenders (Ford Motor Credit, General Motors Acceptance Corp, Toyota Motor Credit, etc.). Owing money to mainstream lenders helps your credit score. A mainstream lender can be one of the aforementioned automobile lenders or a bank.

6) Find a Cosigner for Your Next Auto Purchase

The strength of a borrower's credit helps a lender decide favorably when it comes to loaning money. When you are reestablishing your credit, the lender may want you to find someone—usually a friend or family member with good credit—who will join in the loan process. This can be good for several reasons. First, you will get a lower interest rate, and second, you will obtain a loan from a mainstream lender. If you make your payments on time while you work on your credit, chances are that your credit score will vastly improve. Once your score gets close to 700, it will be much easier to get a loan on your own or possibly refinance your cosigned loan into your name only.

7) Don't Give Up

If at first you don't succeed, try, try again. This maxim applies to disputing credit. If you are certain that a negative item is incorrect and you do not succeed in removing it in your first dispute, repeat the dispute process. In your follow-up disputes, state clearly why you believe a negative item should be removed. Support this with as much documentation as possible, such as receipts, bank statements, and canceled checks.

8) Contact Original Creditor

A number of years ago, I had a negative trade line from a major oil-company gas card on my credit report. It appeared as a charged-off account. I contacted the company and explained that I had been laid off, that I had suffered financially, that my life had turned around, and that I was trying to purchase a home for my new family. I added that my home loan was contingent on my credit score's being just a bit higher than it was. I politely requested that they remove the negative trade line, and low and behold, they did! It never hurts to ask!

9) Settling Your Collection Debt

Collection companies often have the power to reduce the amount you owe. Sometimes, this reduced payoff amount will show up as "settled for less than as agreed" on your

credit reports. This looks bad on your report. When you negotiate the reduced payment, don't forget to include a requirement that the collection company remove the item entirely from your credit reports. If they agree to the reduction,
be prepared to pay the agreed-to amount, but not until you a
document that reflects the deal in writing, with the item's removal expressly included. You may use this documentation
later for a dispute if the collection company does not hold up
its end of the bargain.

10) Using a Secured Credit Card as a Jumpstart to Good Credit

Many people are faced with the hard truth of credit denial.
When I started my credit-recovery process, secured credit
cards did not exist. Securing a credit card merely means that
the borrower must deposit money up front with the credit-
card issuer. Essentially, then, with a secured credit card, you
borrow your own money and pay it back. This reflects on
your credit report as a positive trade line, as long as you
maintain the account in good standing. Some secured credit
cards report to the credit-reporting agencies just like unsecured cards, and they are the most desirable. You can call the
toll-free number found on most secured-credit-card applications and ask if the card's activity is reported like a secured
or an unsecured card. This type of reporting activity will
move you toward obtaining lower-interest-rate credit cards
that are unsecured.

11) Adding a Consumer Statement

You are allowed to add a one-hundred-word statement to your credit reports. You should use this only as a last resort. If you know a negative trade line to be incorrect, or you are unable to resolve the matter, this is your chance to tell your side of the story.

Example Consumer Statement: "I bought a car on April 21st, 2004, from ABC Motors. On April 30th, 2004, the car's engine exploded. I was told that ABC Motors would do nothing. I received a thirty-day warranty when I bought the car. I returned the car to the company's lot, and I shall have no further dealings with them." You will find a template in the *Recreditpair* Letter Generator to help you write your Consumer Statement. (See Letter Requesting the Addition of a Consumer Statement in Part IX, Sample Letters).

12) Keeping Old Positive Accounts Open

Closing credit accounts that have positive histories is a mistake, even if you are not using them any longer. Removing older positive accounts will lower your credit scores. Part of solving the credit-scoring puzzle is to create a strong credit history. An older account strengthens the history on your credit reports.

13) Pay on Time

Once you have started the credit-improvement process, late payments, charge-offs, and collections can be the kiss of death. Lenders look for behavior patterns. If you turn your credit around and then backslide into old habits, this exhibits an unfavorable trend to potential lenders. When making payments, allow seven days if you mail the payment and four days for electronic payment. Ignore any grace periods. At this point, the days of grace periods are over!

14) Keep a Good Mix of Credit

The complicated formula that the credit bureaus use to determine your credit scores takes all of your accounts into consideration. Having a balanced amount of installment and revolving credit is best.

15) Retail Credit Cards

Having credit cards with low limits is the best way to start out in the credit-building process. Retail cards, like secured credit cards, give you an opportunity to build credit and keep balances low. Your goal should always be to establish credit that you can manage and pay as agreed. You should pay your credit cards down below 30 percent of the balance every month.

16) Verify, Verify, Verify

Your new credit knowledge will make it easier for you to obtain and understand your credit reports. You should ensure that no negative information has been added to your credit reports, and you also should verify that no positive accounts have been deleted or have become outdated.

17) Make Sure Your Future Lenders Report to All Major Credit Bureaus

Many people make the mistake of buying their cars from buy-here-pay-here lots. Buy-here-pay-here lots are businesses run by automobile dealers who collect the payments at the dealership. Normally, these organizations do not report the payment activity to the credit-reporting agencies. Some credit unions also do not report to the credit-reporting agencies. Ask questions before borrowing. Don't be in a hurry to take on debt that will not help your credit scores.

18) Fair and Accurate Credit Transaction Act of 2003 (FACT Act or FACTA)

The Fair and Accurate Credit Transaction Act of 2003 (FACT Act or FACTA) is legislation that basically outlines the provisions for consumers' rights in credit transactions. Some of the situations covered by FACTA include account accuracy, limits on information sharing, identify-theft protection, and privacy. You should become familiar with your rights as reflected in this important document. The *Recreditpair* software provides a hyperlink to FACTA.

19) Limit Your Disputes

Never dispute more than three inaccurate accounts per letter. This helps you avoid being accused of filing "frivolous disputes." The credit-reporting agencies may view sending too many disputes in a single letter as frivolous. If a dispute is deemed frivolous, the credit-reporting agencies must notify you of their decision to classify it as such.

20) Free Credit Reports

The AnnualCreditReport.com website (located at www.annualcreditreport.com) allows you to obtain one free credit report per year. You are also entitled to a free credit report if you are denied credit. I recommend that during your first year of working on repairing your credit you review your credit reports on a regular basis, ideally every 60 days.

21) Paid Collections

It would be wonderful if all collection companies would remove their collection trade lines from your credit reports when they are paid, but unfortunately, they are not required to do so. They are required, however, to report settled or satisfied collections as paid. If you find paid collections listed as unpaid on your credit report, you should start the dispute process.

22) Keep Your Inquiries in Check

Seeking a good deal or the most favorable interest rate is a noble goal, but too many inquiries will hurt your credit score. To avoid this problem, confine your shopping to a two-week period. This way your inquiries will not affect your current credit score. Although inquiries remain on your credit reports for two years, only those made in the past twelve months affect your credit score.

23) File Disputes the Old-fashioned Way

You can dispute negative trade lines either electronically over the Internet or manually by using the sample letters in Part IX of this book. I prefer the manual method, and I recommend sending correspondence by Certified Mail with a Return Receipt for all dispute communications. This gives a better paper trail and allows you to start the clock running on the 30-day-response time required of the credit-reporting agencies. I am suspicious of electronic filing because the information is too easily deleted or lost.

See the Mailing-Instructions subsection in Part III for some details regarding mailing. The USPS website, located at www.usps.com, provides in-depth information about mailing options, proof of mailing, tracking, and proof of delivery.

24) Know How to Speak to a Collection-Agency Representative

Allowing your emotions to rule your responses when you communicate with collection-agency representatives is never wise. Granted, these individuals can be over zealous and at times abusive. Add in a dash of your own frustration, and you have a recipe for disaster. If the person with whom you are speaking takes an immovable position with respect to your account, calmly ask to speak to a supervisor. Point out that what you want to accomplish will likely require upper-management approval and that you would like to work on the problem at that level.

25) Paid as Agreed

When paying a charged-off account or a collection account, you have some negotiating power to positively affect your credit report. All creditors, be they original creditors or collection agencies, want their accounts paid. Whether you're paying the full amount or a reduced, agreed-to sum, the time to use your leverage to improve your credit report is during the negotiation. Ask that a "paid-as-agreed" note be added to your credit report. You'll be pleasantly surprised when the creditor or collection agency agrees to carry out your request. Remember, once you pay, your negotiating leverage diminishes dramatically. It's imperative that you insist on any changes to your credit report during the negotiation, i.e., before you pay.

PART IX

PART IX

Sample Letters

You now have all the tools you need to build a good credit score. I could continue to encourage you to persevere, and I could share more of the "secrets" of the credit-reporting agencies, but the truth is that you have what you need in order to proceed. Now, it's up to you to carry the torch across the finish line. I can assure you, though, that your energy, resolve, and determination will win the day.

I suggest that you set aside a quiet afternoon devoted to improving your credit score. Follow the steps in this book, and take your time. Be thorough, thoughtful, and persistent, and you will succeed.

To further help you on the road to achieving a good credit score, I've included some sample letters that you will also find in the Letter Generator of the Recreditpair software. These letters are your major weapons to take into the credit-improvement battle. You should be aware, however, that the letters are examples and must be customized to fit your specific circumstances. Using them verbatim may not be so effective or powerful as tailoring them to your situation. They should serve as models and inspire you to create your own correspondence that will address your specific problem in the most effective way possible. Customizing your letters will make them stronger and reduce the risk of your dispute's being categorized as frivolous.

You'll notice that the letters contain little fluff. I've drafted them that way intentionally, because the folks on the receiving end are busy and not inclined to read wordy, circuitous paragraphs in search of the letter's substance. In your customized version, you should get to the point as quickly as possible, while providing all the necessary information. Below are samples of some letters that I recommend:

Incorrect-Listings Letter

Date

Equifax Information Services
P.O. Box 740256
Atlanta, GA 30374-0256

     RE: Credit-Report Number:
           Credit-Report Date:

Dear Equifax:

Upon reviewing my Equifax credit report, I have discovered some incorrect listings. I enclose a copy of the report and have highlighted the accounts in question.

The following accounts are not mine:

    1. ABC Credit Card
       Account Number: 1234567890

    2. XYZ Company
       Account Number 0987654321

Please verify this dispute with the creditors listed. Once you have done this and have confirmed that I am correct, please remove these accounts from my credit report. I also request that you send me an updated copy of my Equifax credit report showing that these corrections have been made. Thank you.

Sincerely,

John Q. Public
12345 Main Street
Pleasantville, ST 00000
555-555-5555

Outdated-Listings Letter

Date

Experian
National Consumers Assistance Center
P.O. Box 2104
Allen, TX 75013-2104

      RE: Credit-Report Number:
            Credit-Report Date:

Dear Experian:

I have discovered some listings on my current Experian credit report that are outdated. These accounts adversely affect my credit, and I request that they be removed. The following accounts are outdated:

    1. ABC Credit Card
       Account Number: 1234567890

    2. XYZ Company
       Account Number 0987654321

Once you have confirmed that these accounts are outdated, please remove them from my credit report and send me an updated copy of the report showing their deletion. Thank you.

Sincerely,

John Q. Public
12345 Main Street
Pleasantville, ST 00000
555-555-5555

Personal-Information-Errors Letter

Date

TransUnion
Consumer Disclosure Center
P.O. Box 2000
Chester, PA 19022-2000

RE: Credit-Report Number:
Credit-Report Date:

Dear TransUnion,

I recently obtained my TransUnion credit report. The personal-information section contains errors that I would like to have corrected. The following information is incorrect and should be changed:

EXISTING INFORMATION: [INSERT THE ERRONEOUS INFORMATION AS IT APPEARS IN YOUR CREDIT REPORT.]

SHOULD BE CHANGED TO: [FILL IN THE CORRECT INFORMATION.]

Please correct these items and send me an updated credit report showing that the corrections have been made. Thank you.

Sincerely,

John Q. Public
12345 Main Street
Pleasantville, ST 00000
555-555-5555

Investigation-Request Letter

Date

Equifax Information Services
P.O. Box 740256
Atlanta, GA 30374-0256

> RE: Credit-Report Number:
>   Credit-Report Date:

Dear Equifax:

Upon reviewing my current Equifax credit report, I have discovered some questionable items. Please investigate the following listings:

1. ABC Credit Card
   Account Number: 1234567890

2. XYZ Company
   Account Number 0987654321

I am confident that once you complete an investigation with the creditors that have reported this information, I shall be proven correct and you will correct or remove these listings. Once the erroneous items are corrected or removed from my Equifax credit report, please provide me with an updated copy of the report. Thank you.

Sincerely,

John Q. Public
12345 Main Street
Pleasantville, ST 00000
555-555-5555

Request for Item Verification

Date

TransUnion
Consumer Disclosure Center
P.O. Box 2000
Chester, PA 19022-2000

> RE: Credit-Report Number:
> Credit-Report Date:

Dear TransUnion:

I have received my TransUnion credit report and have discovered items that need verification. The accuracy of my credit report is important to me. Please verify that the information is correct for the following listings:

> 1. ABC Credit Card
>   Account Number: 1234567890
>
> 2. XYZ Company
>   Account Number 0987654321

Verifying that the above-listed items belong on my credit report is your obligation under federal law. I appreciate your reviewing these items and verifying the accuracy of the information reflected in them. I look forward to receiving your reply confirming that these listings have been corrected or removed from my credit report. Thank you.

Sincerely,

John Q. Public
12345 Main Street
Pleasantville, ST 00000
555-555-5555

Wrong-Account Letter #1

Date

Equifax Information Services
P.O. Box 740256
Atlanta, GA 30374-0256

RE: Credit-Report Number:
Credit-Report Date:

Dear Equifax:

This letter shall serve as my formal complaint regarding errors on my credit report. The account listed below is not mine. I have no knowledge of it. This account is damaging to my credit and must be removed from my credit report. I request that the following account be investigated and removed from my file:

ABC Credit Card
Account Number: 1234567890

Please provide me with the names and business addresses of the persons whom you contact for verification of this information. I also demand to see any document that bears my signature requesting an account with the above-named company. Federal law requires you to respond within 30 days of your receipt of my complaint. The Federal Trade Commission (see 15 USC 41, et seq) investigates failures by credit-reporting agencies to comply with federal regulations. I am maintaining a careful record of my communications with you on this matter in preparation for filing a complaint with the FTC.

Please delete the misleading information from my credit report and supply a corrected credit profile to all creditors who have received a copy of my credit report within the last six months and to all entities that have received a copy of my credit report for employment purposes within the past two years. Also, please send me an updated copy of my credit report showing that the item has been deleted.

Sincerely,

John Q. Public
12345 Main Street
Pleasantville, ST 00000
555-555-5555

Wrong-Account Letter #2

Date

Experian
National Consumers Assistance Center
P.O. Box 2104
Allen, TX 75013-2104

> RE: Credit-Report Number:
>   Credit-Report Date:

Dear Experian:

I write this letter to formally request that you verify some of the accounts that are listed on my Experian credit report. I have no memory of these accounts, and I request proof of verification. By law, you have 30 days to verify these items. If you are unable to do so, you must remove the listings from my credit report. I enclose a copy of my Experian credit report with the following questionable accounts highlighted:

> 1. ABC Credit Card
>   Account Number: 1234567890
>
> 2. XYZ Company
>   Account Number 0987654321

After you determine that these accounts are inaccurate and should not appear on my Equifax credit report, please remove them and forward an updated copy of the report to me as soon as possible. I appreciate your prompt attention to this mater. Thank you.

Sincerely,

John Q. Public
12345 Main Street
Pleasantville, ST 00000
555-555-5555

Request for Verification of Disputed Items

Date

TransUnion
Consumer Disclosure Center
P.O. Box 2000
Chester, PA 19022-2000

      RE: Credit-Report Number:
             Credit-Report Date:

Dear TransUnion:

I write this to officially request that you verify questionable items that I have discovered on my TransUnion credit report. According to federal law, you are required to prove that these items are accurately reflected on my report. Please review the attached copy of my TransUnion credit report and investigate the following items:

    1. ABC Credit Card
       Account Number: 1234567890

    2. XYZ Company
       Account Number 0987654321.

I have highlighted on the report the items to be verified. Federal law requires that you complete your investigation within 30 days and send me an updated copy of my credit report.

I look forward to receiving your reply. Thank you.

Sincerely,

John Q. Public
12345 Main Street
Pleasantville, ST 00000
555-555-5555

Request to Remove Inaccuracies

Date

Equifax Information Services
P.O. Box 740256
Atlanta, GA 30374-0256

      RE: Credit-Report Number:
            Credit-Report Date:

Dear Equifax:

I have obtained a copy of my Equifax credit report, and I have discovered an alarming number of inaccuracies listed under my name. I would like you to please confirm and verify that the following items are correct. I enclose a copy of my Equifax credit report with the questionable accounts highlighted. Please investigate the following items:

    1. ABC Credit Card
       Account Number: 1234567890

    2. XYZ Company
       Account Number 0987654321

Please forward a revised copy of my credit report to me when your investigation is complete. Thank you.

Sincerely,

John Q. Public
12345 Main Street
Pleasantville, ST 00000
555-555-5555

Review-Request Letter

Date

Experian
National Consumers Assistance Center
P.O. Box 2104
Allen, TX 75013-2104

> RE: Credit-Report Number:
>   Credit-Report Date:

Dear Experian:

Recently, I received a copy of my Experian credit report and have reviewed my credit status and credit score. I have discovered some items on the report that concern me, and I would like you to verify their accuracy. I have worked hard to keep my credit in good standing, and I understand that you are required, under the provisions of the Fair Credit Reporting Act (FCRA), to verify the accuracy of questionable information that appears in my credit report. Please review the following items:

1. ABC Credit Card
   Account Number: 1234567890

2. XYZ Company
   Account Number 0987654321

Any delay in investigating this matter would certainly damage my credit. Please forward a copy of my updated credit report to me when your investigation is completed. I look forward to receiving your reply.

Thank you for your cooperation and attention to this matter.

Sincerely,

John Q. Public
12345 Main Street
Pleasantville, ST 00000
555-555-5555

Requesting-Proof Letter #1

Date

TransUnion
Consumer Disclosure Center
P.O. Box 2000
Chester, PA 19022-2000

>   RE: Credit-Report Number:
>   Credit-Report Date:

Dear TransUnion:

Recently, I received a copy of my TransUnion credit report, and upon reviewing it, I have discovered some items that are reflected incorrectly on the report. Please verify the accuracy of the following accounts:

>   1. ABC Credit Card
>   Account Number: 1234567890
>
>   2. XYZ Company
>   Account Number 0987654321

According to federal law, you are obligated to review my credit report and correct or delete any items that appear in error. If you find that the above-listed items are incorrect, please remove them, update my credit report, and forward to me an updated copy of the report showing the removal of these accounts. Thank you.

Sincerely,

John Q. Public
12345 Main Street
Pleasantville, ST 00000
555-555-5555

Requesting-Proof Letter #2

Date

Equifax Information Services
P.O. Box 740256
Atlanta, GA 30374-0256

      RE: Credit-Report Number:
              Credit-Report Date:

Dear Equifax:

Under the Fair Credit Reporting Act, I have the right to request verification of information contained on my credit report. Please verify the following listings:

1. ABC Credit Card
   Account Number: 1234567890

2. XYZ Company
   Account Number 0987654321

Once you have completed your investigation and verification, please send a copy of the corrected credit report to me at the following address:

John Q. Public
12345 Main Street
Pleasantville, ST 00000

Thank you for your assistance.

Sincerely,

John Q. Public
12345 Main Street
Pleasantville, ST 00000
555-555-5555

Request for Removal of a Specific Item

Date

Experian
National Consumers Assistance Center
P.O. Box 2104
Allen, TX 75013-2104

> RE: Credit-Report Number:
>   Credit-Report Date:

Dear Experian:

I have done some research and have learned that you are legally responsible to investigate and remove items from a credit report if the items are unverifiable. I believe the following items do not belong on my credit report, and I request that you verify them:

1. ABC Credit Card
   Account Number: 1234567890

2. XYZ Company
   Account Number 0987654321

Once you have completed your investigation and verification, please send a copy of the corrected credit report to me at the following address:

John Q. Public
12345 Main Street
Pleasantville, ST 00000

Thank you for your prompt assistance.

Sincerely,

John Q. Public
12345 Main Street
Pleasantville, ST 00000
555-555-5555

Request for Description of Procedures

Date

TransUnion
Consumer Disclosure Center
P.O. Box 2000
Chester, PA 19022-2000

      RE: Credit-Report Number:
            Credit-Report Date:

Dear TransUnion:

This letter is a formal request for a description of the procedures used to determine the accuracy and completeness of accounts I am disputing. Please include the business name, address, and telephone number of any person or entity that furnishes information in connection with this reinvestigation.

You have failed to employ reasonable procedures to assure complete accuracy with respect to the information you publish. Please reinvestigate the accuracy of the following accounts and remove them from my credit report:

    1. ABC Credit Card
       Account Number: 1234567890

    2. XYZ Company
       Account Number 0987654321

Please send a corrected credit report to all creditors who have received a copy of my credit report within the last six months and to all employers who have received the report within the past two years. Thank you.

Sincerely,

John Q. Public
12345 Main Street
Pleasantville, ST 00000
555-555-5555

Follow-up General-Complaint Letter

Date

Equifax Information Services
P.O. Box 740256
Atlanta, GA 30374-0256

> RE: Credit-Report Number:
>   Credit-Report Date:

Dear Equifax,

More than 30 days have passed since I formally registered a complaint with you. Although federal law requires that you respond to my complaint within 30 days of receiving it, you have failed to respond. I attach a copy of my original letter to you as well as a copy of my Equifax credit report with the errors highlighted.

Your delay has had a decidedly negative effect on my credit standing. Please complete your verification and remove the disputed items from my credit report. The following accounts are in question:

> 1. ABC Credit Card
>   Account Number: 1234567890
>
> 2. XYZ Company
>   Account Number 0987654321

Thank you for your prompt attention to this urgent matter.

Sincerely,

John Q. Public
12345 Main Street
Pleasantville, ST 00000
555-555-5555

Incorrect-Inquiries Letter

Date

Experian
National Consumers Assistance Center
P.O. Box 2104
Allen, TX 75013-2104

     RE: Credit-Report Number:
           Credit-Report Date:

Dear Experian:

I recently received a copy of my Experian credit report. Upon reviewing it, I have discovered some inquires that I do not recall authorizing. I request that you investigate the following listings:

    1. ABC Credit Card
       Date of Inquiry

    2. XYZ Company
       Date of Inquiry

Please provide me with a document bearing my signature proving that I applied for such credit. If you are unable to do so, please delete the above-listed inquires from my Experian credit report and send me an updated credit report showing that the corrections have been made. Thank you.

Sincerely,

John Q. Public
12345 Main Street
Pleasantville, ST 00000
555-555-5555

Follow-up Dispute Letter

Date

TransUnion
Consumer Disclosure Center
P.O. Box 2000
Chester, PA 19022-2000

      RE: Credit-Report Number:
              Credit-Report Date:

Dear TransUnion:

I have not received a response from you regarding my dispute letter dated (fill in date). Federal law requires that you respond within 30 days of receiving my complaint. Your failure to comply with federal regulations may be investigated by the Federal Trade Commission (please see 15 USC 41, et seq.). I am maintaining a careful record of my communications with you on this matter for the purpose of filing a complaint with the FTC. The following information must be verified or deleted from my credit report:

      1. ABC Credit Card
         Account Number: 1234567890

      2. XYZ Company
         Account Number 0987654321

As I emphasized in my earlier dispute letter, the above-listed items are inaccurate. Please delete these accounts and supply a corrected credit report to all creditors who have received a copy of my credit report within the last six months and to all employers who have received the report within the past two years.

I also request that a description of the procedure used to determine the accuracy and completeness of the information be provided to me within 15 days of the completion of your reinvestigation. Thank you.

Sincerely,

John Q. Public
12345 Main Street
Pleasantville, ST 00000
555-555-5555

Letter Requesting the Addition of a Consumer Statement

Date

Equifax Information Services
P.O. Box 740256
Atlanta, GA 30374-0256

   RE: Credit-Report Number:
      Credit-Report Date:

Dear Equifax

The following paragraph is a Consumer Statement, and I request that you include it in my credit report as soon as possible:

[Insert your consumer statement of fewer than 100 words here. State the name of the creditor, the date the account was reported, and the amount of the disputed debt. Then state the facts that support your argument for not having paid the bill. Be complete, but brief.]

Thank you for including this consumer statement in my credit report. If you have any questions, please contact me in writing at 12345 Main Street, Pleasantville, ST 00000 or by telephone at 555-555-5555. Thank you.

Sincerely,

John Q. Public
12345 Main Street
Pleasantville, ST 00000
555-555-5555

PART X

PART X

Glossary

ABA Routing Number:

An ABA Routing Number is a nine-digit code that appears at the bottom of negotiable instruments, such as checks, and is used to identify specific accounts at banks and other financial institutions. It is also used to effect bank-to-bank wire transfers.

Adjustable-Rate Mortgage (ARM):

An adjustable-rate mortgage is a mortgage with an interest rate that varies in accordance with some external standard, such as the prime rate, the interest rate on United-States-Treasury securities, or the inflation rate. ARMs may have limits (caps) on how much their interest rates can rise or fall.

Adjustment Period:

The adjustment period is the time between adjustment dates for an adjustable-rate mortgage.

Adverse Account:

This term is used by lenders and credit agencies and consists of any account that is delinquent for more than 30 days.

Age Requirement:

In order to qualify for credit, you must be at least 18 years old, or a parent or guardian must cosign the loan agreement.

AKA:

This is an acronym for "also known as." It includes business names, maiden names, and spelling variations of names.

Alias:

This is similar to aka. If you have used two or more names on your financial accounts, your aliases will show up on your credit report.

Amortization:

Amortization is the process of spreading a debt over a period of time and scheduling regular payments that reduce it. Typically, lenders amortize automobile loans and mortgages for more orderly payment.

AnnualCreditReport.com:

AnnualCreditReport.com   (www.annualcreditreport.com) is the official website for obtaining free credit-report disclosures from Equifax, Experian, and TransUnion. Under FACTA regulations, you have a right to request your credit reports online, by telephone, or by regular mail once a year for no fee. This free service does not include credit scores or credit-monitoring services.

Annual Fee:

Some credit-card companies charge annual fees, which are the fees you pay each year to use the card. It's best to seek credit-card companies that do not charge fees to use their cards.

Annual Percentage Rate (APR):

When you open a credit-card account, you agree to pay a percentage of the outstanding balance each month as a finance charge. The annual percentage rate is the rate of interest that a credit-card company charges you, expressed on an annualized basis.

Annual Percentage Yield (APY):

The annual percentage yield is the rate of interest earned by an account owner over the course of a year.

Application for Credit:

This is the application form used to seek credit. Filling one out usually prompts an inquiry into your credit status.

Application Fee:

Some lenders charge a fee for processing their loan applications.

Application Scoring:

Application scoring is a numerical system that businesses use to evaluate a credit applicant's loan risk. It takes into account a variety of factors, such as employment and income history.

Appraisal Fee:

An appraisal fee is charged for estimating the value of property offered as security for a loan. This fee can range from hundreds of dollars for an appraisal of a normal house or condominium to several thousand dollars for appraising higher-value property in some areas of the country.

Appraised Value:

This term refers to an assessment of the value of a piece of property based on the expert opinion of the appraiser. Factors an appraiser may take into consideration include the price of similar properties in the area, the condition of the property, and any special features of the property.

Appraisal:

An appraisal is the written report that estimates of the value of a property.

Appraiser:

An appraiser is a trained inspector who estimates the value of property.

Appreciation:

Appreciation is the increase in the value of a property.

Asset:

An asset consists of cash or property that can be turned into cash. Real property, goods, savings, and investments are different asset forms.

Assumable Mortgage:

An assumable mortgage is one that allows a purchaser to step into the place of a seller in order to assume a loan under the same terms and conditions that apply to the seller.

Assumption:

An assumption is the act of assuming the responsibility for a mortgage. A purchaser who engages in the assumption of a mortgage takes over the seller's responsibilities as set forth in the seller's mortgage agreement.

Assumption Clause:

An assumption clause allows a buyer to assume a seller's mortgage. A natural result of an assumption is that the loan need not be paid in full by the original borrower.

Assumption Fee:

If a purchaser assumes an existing mortgage, the lender will require the payment of an assumption fee.

Authorized User:

An authorized user is a person who is authorized to use the credit card or credit account of another person. The credit-card company will usually issue a separate card with the authorized user's name on it. An authorized user is not legally responsible for the debt incurred on the card; rather, the principal cardholder retains that full responsibility. The authorized user's name is reported to the credit-reporting agencies, however, and if the debt is paid on time, the authorized user's credit will improve along with that of the principal cardholder.

Available Credit:

The available credit is the amount of unused credit that is available on your credit card, credit account, or credit line. Your available credit consists of the balance outstanding subtracted from your total credit limit.

B

Bad Credit:

Bad credit occurs as a result of making late payments, missing payments, exceeding the limits on credit cards, defaulting on loans, or declaring bankruptcy.

Balance/Amount Owed:

This is the amount you owe a creditor. It includes any unpaid balance from the previous month, new purchases, cash advances, and charges such as annual fees, late fees, and finance charges.

Balance-Calculation Method:

This is a system used by credit-card issuers to calculate balances owed and the interest due each month.

Balance Sheet:

A balance sheet is a financial report that states the value of your assets, liabilities, and net worth as of a specific date.

Balance Transfer:

A balance transfer is the movement of debt from one credit card to another. The point of taking such action is usually to obtain a lower interest rate. Balance transfers can also be made for other types of financial accounts.

Balloon Mortgage:

A balloon mortgage is a mortgage that is to be repaid in regularly scheduled payments over a fixed period and requires a lump-sum payment of the remaining principal at the end of that period.

Balloon Payment:

A balloon payment is the final payment on a balloon mortgage. The payment consists of a lump-sum amount that is paid at the end of the loan period.

Bankrupt:

An individual or entity that has declared bankruptcy.

Bankruptcy:

When debtors can no longer meet their current debt-payment obligations, they may declare bankruptcy, which affords them relief from their debts in exchange for surrendering their assets to a court-appointed trustee. Declaring bankruptcy will damage your credit for up to ten years, and should only be undertaken as a last resort. Two types of bankruptcy are most common for individuals—Chapter 7 and Chapter 13. Federal-tax debt, student loans, and child support are exempt from bankruptcy protection, which means that the obligation to pay remains after the bankruptcy.

Bankruptcy Code:

The Bankruptcy Code is a federal law governing the conditions and procedures under which persons claiming an inability to repay their debts can seek relief.

Beacon Score:

This is the credit-scoring system used by the credit-reporting agency Equifax.

Basis Point:

A basis point is 1/100th of a percentage point. A fee calculated as ten basis points of a $200,000 loan would be 0.10 percent, or $200.

Before-Tax Income:

Before-tax income is a taxpayer's total income before deducting taxes.

Beneficiary:

A beneficiary is a person designated to receive income or other benefits from an insurance policy, trust, estate, or deed of trust.

Binder:

This is a preliminary agreement under which a buyer offers to purchase real estate and secures the offer with an earnest-money deposit.

Biweekly Mortgage:

A biweekly mortgage is a mortgage that is paid in scheduled payments every two weeks. Most mortgages are paid monthly, but biweekly mortgages can often save homeowners money, because the payment schedule creates the rough equivalent of an extra monthly payment, which the mortgage company applies entirely against the principal.

Breach:

A breach is the violation of a contract or other legal obligation.

Bridge Loan:

This is a loan that is secured by the borrower's current home, which is usually for sale. It allows the loan proceeds to be used for closing costs on a new house prior to the sale of the current home.

Broker:

A broker is a person who, for a fee or commission, brings parties together and helps them negotiate a contract. In real-estate transactions, the broker typically represents the seller, but a broker or real-estate agent may represent a buyer by executing a buyer-agent agreement, which stipulates that the buyer pay the broker's sales commission.

Broker Premium:

This is a fee paid to the mortgage broker for bringing the lender and the borrower together. In general, mortgage brokers obtain discounted loans from financial institutions and then mark up the price to the borrower. The difference between the marked-up price and the discounted price is the broker premium.

Borrower:

This is the person applying for a loan and who is responsible for paying it back.

C

Call Option:

A call option is a provision in a mortgage that allows the lender to declare the mortgage due and payable (call the mortgage) at the end of a specified period of time for any reason.

Cap:

A cap is clause in an adjustable-rate-mortgage contract that limits the frequency of interest-rate changes, the amount the interest rate can change in any one period, and/or the amount the interest rate can vary over the life of the loan.

Capital Improvement:

A capital improvement is the addition of something to real property that increases its value. Some examples are: upgrading a kitchen, erecting a new garage, adding a bedroom, and landscaping a yard.

Capacity:

A lender assesses a potential borrower's capacity by weighing present income and the probability of continuing to receive it against the amount of debt the borrower is carrying at the time of submission of the credit application. Capacity is a significant factor in a lender's determination of a borrower's creditworthiness.

Cardholder:

A cardholder is someone to whom a credit-card company has issued a credit card. Other individuals who are authorized to use the same account are also cardholders.

Cash Advance:

A cash advance is a cash loan you received from a lender. These loans often carry higher-than-normal interest rates based on the amount of the advance. Most cash advances are for $500 or less.

Certificate of Deposit:

Commonly known as a "CD," a certificate of deposit has a maturity date and a specified rate of interest. Cashing in a certificate of deposit before its maturity date usually draws a penalty.

Certificate of Eligibility:

A Certificate of Eligibility is a document issued by the federal government to a veteran of military service certifying that person's eligibility for a Department-of-Veterans-Affairs (VA) mortgage.

Certificate of Reasonable Value (CRV):

This is a Department-of-Veterans-Affairs document that establishes a limit on the maximum VA loan value. Its issuance is based on an appraisal of the property.

Chain of Title:

The chain of title is the legal history of the title to a parcel of real property. All transfers of the property are recorded in chronological order.

Chapter 7 Bankruptcy:

Chapter 7 is a section of the Federal Bankruptcy Code that provides for a court-supervised sale of the assets of a financially troubled individual or entity. This form of bankruptcy does not require the payment of debts that were owed before filing. A record of the bankruptcy remains on your credit report for ten years, and credit accounts that are included in your Chapter 7 proceeding remain on your credit report for seven years.

Chapter 11 Bankruptcy:

Chapter 11 bankruptcies are usually filed by entities seeking re-lief from the pursuit of creditors. The proceeding results in the restructuring of the outstanding debt with a view toward the debtor's eventual payment of some or all of it. Since the U.S. Supreme Court has held that an individual may also use Chapter 11, the provision serves as an alternative to Chapter 7.

Chapter 12 Bankruptcy:

This form of bankruptcy is designed specifically for farmers and fishermen. Cases filed under this provision are adminis-tered like Chapter 11 proceedings, but they include special protections tailored to the unique situations in which family farms and fishing operations find themselves.

Chapter 13 Bankruptcy:

This type of bankruptcy allows the debtor to pay outstanding debts in installments. A Chapter 13 bankruptcy remains on your credit report for seven years from the discharge date. If the filing is not discharged, the record remains on your report for ten years from the original filing date. Each credit account discharged through this type of bankruptcy proceed-ing remains on your credit report for seven years.

Charge-Off:

When a creditor makes a final decision not to continue pur-suing the payment of an outstanding debt, it will execute a charge-off of the debt amount. A charge-off does not re-lieve the debtor of the account's effect on the credit score.

Although the debt has been charged off, the credit-reporting agencies still view it as an unsatisfied obligation. Accounts that have been charged off remain on your credit report for seven years and will harm your credit score. Even after being charged off, the creditor can sell the account to a collection agency.

Claim Amount:

An amount demanded by a party to a civil lawsuit.

Clear Title:

This term refers to a title to real property that is free of liens and legal questions.

Closing:

Also called a "settlement," the closing is the final step of the sale of real property. It includes the execution of mortgage instruments and the payment of closing costs.

Closing Costs:

Closing costs are fees paid by a borrower when transferring ownership of a property, receiving a loan for the purchase of a property, or refinancing an existing loan for a property.

Collateral:

Collateral is any asset of value that is used to secure a loan.

Collateral Inspection:

Collateral inspections are progress inspections ordered by a lender to ensure that the construction of a home or other property improvement is proceeding according to plan.

Closing Statement:

This is the final statement of the amount and allocation of costs incurred to complete a loan for the purchase of real property.

Collection:

This is the referral of a past-due account to an individual or organization that specializes in collecting unpaid debts. A creditor will often sell the debt for a reduced amount to a collection agency that will work to recover the amount owed. This usually occurs after an account is over 180 days past due. Collection records may remain on your credit report for seven years from the date of the last 180-day-late payment on the original debt.

Collection Agency:

A collection agency is a company that specializes in recovering past-due debts by contacting borrowers by telephone and mail. The Fair Debt Collection Practices Act (FDCPA) defines debtors' rights in the collection process.

Co-maker:

A co-maker (cosigner) is sometimes used in situations where a loan applicant's qualifications are questionable. A co-maker usually has a strong credit history and assumes responsibility to pay if the borrower fails to do so. In the event that the borrower does not pay, the co-maker becomes legally responsible to make the payments.

Commercial Bank:

A commercial bank is a bank that accepts deposits and makes loans primarily to businesses.

Commitment Fee:

The fee paid by a borrower to a lender in exchange for a promise to keep a credit line open under agreed-to terms for a set period of time.

Commission:

A real-estate broker or agent who completes a negotiation for a real-estate transaction typically charges a commission based on a percentage of the sale price of the property.

Commitment Letter:

Also known as a "Loan Commitment," a Commitment Letter is a formal offer made by a lender that specifies the terms of the anticipated loan.

Comparables:

Real-estate appraisers utilize comparables (also referred to as "comparable properties" or "comps") to assist in determining the approximate fair-market value of the property under consideration.

Compound Interest:

Compound interest is the process of adding interest earned on an account to the principal amount so that interest is earned on that interest from that point forward.

Construction Loan:

A construction loan is a short-term real-estate loan designed for financing construction costs. During the execution of the construction project, the loan funds are disbursed as needed or in accordance with a prearranged schedule. Upon the project's completion, the money is repaid from the proceeds of a mortgage loan. The interest rate on the construction loan is usually higher than the prime rate, and the loan agreement often includes an origination fee.

Consumer Credit:

Consumer credit is credit extended to an individual that permits the purchase of goods or services. Such personal loans can be secured or unsecured and may include revolving credit.

Consumer Credit Protection Act (CCPA):

The Consumer Credit Protection Act establishes rules of disclosure that lenders must observe in their dealings with borrowers. It stipulates that lenders must inform borrowers of annual percentage rates, potential total costs, and special loan terms. The CCPA is also known as the Truth-in-Lending Act (TILA).

Contingency:

A contingency is a condition that must be met before a contract is legally binding. For example, homebuyers often include a contingency that specifically states that the contract is not binding until the buyer obtains a satisfactory home-inspection report from a qualified home inspector.

Contract:

A contract is an exchange of promises among parties to carry out an agreement enforceable by law. Contracts can be oral or written, although contracts for the sale of real estate must be written.

Convenience Check:

Credit-card companies issue convenience checks (you may have found them in your mailbox) that you can use to access your available credit. These checks often carry interest rates and terms that differ from those of regular credit cards.

Conventional Mortgage:

A mortgage that is not insured or guaranteed by the federal government.

Convertible Adjustable-Rate Mortgage (Convertible ARM):

This is an adjustable-rate mortgage that can be converted to a fixed-rate mortgage under specified conditions.

Cosigner:

A person who signs a loan document along with the borrower and takes equal responsibility for the debt owed. Borrowers often use cosigners if their credit or financial situation does not permit them to qualify for a loan on their own. A cosigner is held legally responsible for the loan, and the joint account will appear on the cosigner's credit report as well.

Covenant:

A covenant is a restriction on a loan document. A violation of one of the covenants in your loan agreement can result in foreclosure.

Credit:

A lender extends you credit for the purchase of something of value in exchange for your promise to repay the lender at a later date. You can charge any amount to your credit line to make purchases or take cash advances. As long as you pay the minimum amount due each month by the due date, you can continue using your remaining available credit.

Credit Bureau (Credit-Reporting Agency):

A credit bureau is a company that collects and sells information about how you manage your credit. Three national credit bureaus—Equifax, Experian, and TransUnion—are the principal players. Many banks and credit issuers regularly report to the credit bureaus about your payment habits and how much money you owe. Potential creditors may check your credit report when you seek to rent an apartment or when you apply for a loan, credit card, or new job. If you are denied credit, the creditor must reveal to you the source of the credit information.

Credit Counseling:

Many nonprofit companies provide credit-counseling services and are both helpful and affordable. In contrast, "credit-repair companies" masquerading as credit counselors are usually expensive and often ineffective.

Credit-Card Debt:

Your credit-card debt is the total unpaid balance on all of your credit cards (not to be confused with the minimum amount you owe each month).

Credit Criteria:

Credit criteria are factors used by lenders to rate an individual's credit worthiness or ability to repay debt. They may include income, amount of personal debt, number of accounts from other credit sources, and credit history. As long as a lender does not violate any of the provisions of the Equal Credit Opportunity Act (ECOA), it is free to use any credit-related information in approving or denying a credit application.

Credit File:

A credit file is a complete record of your credit history, gathered and maintained by a credit bureau.

Credit History:

Your credit history is a record of how you have borrowed and repaid debts. Banks and credit-card issuers report your payment activity to the credit bureaus. When you apply for new credit or a loan, the lender will check your credit history before issuing credit.

Credit Limit:

Your credit limit is the maximum credit you have with a specific lender. In the case of credit cards, it is typically listed on your credit-card bills.

Credit Management:

The way you handle the money you borrow from banks or credit issuers.

Credit Obligation:

A borrower's legal responsibility to pay back borrowed money.

Creditor:

A creditor is any individual or entity that extends credit, such as a merchant, bank, or mortgage lender.

Credit Repair:

This is the reason you purchased this book! You can work on your own credit repair with the help of *Recreditpair*.

Credit Rating:

A credit rating is an evaluation of an individual's or company's credit history and capability of repaying debt. Although many firms investigate, analyze, and maintain credit history, the three principal agencies are Equifax, Experian, and TransUnion. The credit rating is based on the number of outstanding debts and whether they have been repaid in a timely manner in the past. (See Credit Score.)

Credit Report:

A credit report is a record of the information that credit bureaus have collected about the way you've managed your finances over the past seven to ten years. It is an official record of how reliable you are in paying your creditors. It includes the names of companies that have lent you money, your account balances, and the timeliness of your payments. The information on your credit report can either qualify or disqualify you from obtaining credit cards, mortgages, loans, apartment leases, and employment.

Credit-Reporting Agency (Credit Bureau):

This is an organization that prepares credit reports used by lenders to determine a potential borrower's credit history. The agency collects data for its reports from a credit repository as well as from other sources.

Credit Score:

A credit score is a statistical system for assigning numerical values to characteristics related to information in your credit report. It usually ranges from 300 to 850, with 680 or higher considered a good credit score. Many different credit-scoring formulas exist, and each one produces scores that vary slightly from those of the other credit-reporting agencies.

Credit Union:

A credit union is a cooperative financial institution run by its members, consisting of a group of employees, a labor union, or a religious group. Credit Unions may offer a full range of financial services and sometimes pay higher interest rates on deposits and charge lower interest rates on loans than commercial banks.

Creditworthiness:

Creditworthiness is a creditor's measure of a consumer's ability to repay debts.

CURR WAS FOR:

This is a loan abbreviation that indicates that although you have paid all past-due amounts and your account is now current, foreclosure proceedings have already begun.

D

Daily Periodic Rate:

The Daily Periodic Rate is the interest charged on a loan calculated on a daily basis. It is computed by dividing the yearly interest rate by 365.

Debit Card:

When you make a purchase with a debit card, the seller deducts the payment directly from of your bank account. The debit card will allow you to spend only the amount of money in your bank account.

Debt:

The amount of money owed for money, goods, or services.

Debt Consolidation:

A debt consolidation combines your debts into a single loan. You can arrange to do this with a financial institution or through a debt-counseling service. Student loans are often consolidated in order to secure lower interest rates. (See Credit Counseling.)

Debt Counseling:

Debt counseling is the process of getting you back on your financial feet through the assistance of qualified financial experts. Debt counselors assist you by discussing your financial problems with you and negotiating with your creditors.

For example, your debt counselor may convince a lender to spread payments over a longer period in order to reduce the monthly amount due.

Debt Settlement:

This term refers to the settlement of a borrower's debt with a creditor.

Debt-to-Available-Credit Ratio:

Your debt-to-available-credit ratio is the ratio of the amount you owe on a loan to your credit limit. Higher ratios signal higher risk to lenders.

Debt-to-Income Ratio:

Your debt-to-income ratio is the ratio of the amount you owe on a loan to your monthly pretax income.

Deed:

A deed is a legal document that, when delivered, transfers title to property.

Deed in Lieu of Foreclosure:

In order to avoid foreclosure, a purchaser may deliver a deed in lieu of foreclosure to the lender in satisfaction of a debt that is in default.

Deed of Trust:

This document is used instead of a mortgage in some states.

Default:

A default is a failure to repay a loan according to the agreed-upon terms. It has a decidedly negative effect on one's credit score.

Deferred Payment:

Deferred payment delays the obligation to pay or extends it over a longer period of time. During the deferred-payment period, interest usually continues to accumulate.

Delinquency:

Overdue loan payments are referred to as delinquent. Delinquencies remain on your credit report for seven years and damage your credit score.

Direct Deposit:

A direct deposit is an automatic deposit of wages or bonuses into a consumer's bank account.

Dispute:

A dispute is the process of submitting a request to the credit bureaus to correct an error on a credit report. The credit bureaus must investigate the matter and update your credit report within 30 days of receipt of the dispute communication.

Deposit:

A deposit is money delivered by a potential homebuyer showing good faith in the offer to purchase real property. (See Earnest-Money Deposit) It can also be a sum of money that ensures payment or an advance of funds in the processing of a loan.

Depreciation:

This is the amount by which an asset's value falls within a given time period.

Down Payment:

This is a portion of the purchase price of a property that the buyer pays upfront in the transaction.

Due Date:

The due date is the date that a payment is due to a creditor. After that date, the creditor can charge a late fee, record the payment as late, and consider the account delinquent.

E

Earnest-Money Deposit:

An earnest-money deposit is money delivered by a potential homebuyer showing good faith in the offer to purchase real property.

Easement:

An easement is a right-of-way that allows access to or across real property.

Effective Age:

An appraiser's estimate of a property's conditional age (age based on the property's condition rather than its chronological age) is used in determining the property's effective age.

Depending on the condition of property, its actual age may be more or less than its effective age.

Electronic Banking:

Electronic banking is a form of banking where funds are transferred through an exchange of information via the Internet rather than through the exchange of cash or checks. Consumers view their billing information by logging onto their banks' Internet websites. Customer identification is by access code, such as a password or Personal-Identification Number (PIN).

Electronic Bill Pay:

This is Internet-based billing that allows consumers to view and pay credit-card and other retail bills online. Consumers view their billing information on their banks' Internet websites, decide what bills to pay, and authorize payment by electronic mail.

Electronic Checks (e-checks):

Electronic checks are the electronic equivalent to paper checks and are used to pay bills, transfer funds, or accomplish any other purpose for which a paper check could be used.

Electronic-Funds Transfer (EFT):

One can use an electronic-funds transfer to move funds electronically rather than by check.

Empirica Score:

Empirica Score is the name of TransUnion's credit-scoring system. It is one of many slightly differing credit-scoring formulas used by bankers, lenders, creditors, insurers, and retailers.

Equal-Credit Opportunity:

This term refers to a federal law that ensures that you have an equal opportunity to obtain credit. This law protects consumers from credit discrimination based on race, gender, age, marital status, public-assistance income, nationality, or religion.

Equifax:

One of three national credit-reporting agencies that collect and sell consumer-credit-history records to banks and lenders.

Equity:

Your available home equity is the fair-market value of your home less all outstanding mortgage balances. You build equity in a home as you pay down your mortgage and as the property value increases.

Escrow:

An escrow involves depositing with a third party an item of value, money, or documents to be delivered upon the fulfillment of a specific condition.

Escrow Account:

In the sale of a property, a mortgage company holds the borrower's payments in an escrow account prior to paying property expenses.

Estate:

An estate includes all real and personal property. The term is used frequently in connection with the assets of the deceased at the time of death.

Examination of Title:

An examination of title is an investigation and final report regarding the title to a piece of real property and is based on research of the public records.

Experian:

One of three national credit-reporting agencies that collect and sell consumer-credit-history records to banks and lenders.

Expiration Term:

The expiration term is the number of years that a credit record will remain on your credit report (as mandated by the Fair Credit Reporting Act). Most negative records stay on your credit report for seven to ten years. The shortest expiration term is two years for inquiry records. The longest expiration term is 15 years for paid tax liens or indefinitely for unpaid tax liens. Positive information can stay on your credit report indefinitely.

F

Fair and Accurate Credit Transaction Act (FACT Act or FACTA):

FACTA requires credit bureaus to provide each U.S. resident with a free credit report once a year, upon the individual's request. It also includes new privacy regulations, identity-theft protections, and dispute-procedure requirements.

Fair Credit and Charge Card Disclosure Act of 1988:

This federal law ensures that credit and charge-card issuers provide you with the facts necessary to make wise credit decisions.

Fair Credit Billing Act (FCBA):

This federal law ensures that you can find and fix billing mistakes.

Fair Credit Reporting Act (FCRA):

This federal law promotes the accuracy, confidentiality, and proper use of information in the credit files kept by credit-reporting agencies. It specifies the expiration terms for records on your credit report, defines who can access your credit data, and grants consumers the right to view and dispute their credit records.

Fair Debt Collection Practices Act (FDCPA):

This federal law ensures protection from harassment and unfair treatment by debt collectors.

Fair-Market Value:

The fair-market value of property is the price that a buyer is willing to pay and that a seller is willing to accept, assuming that neither buyer nor seller is desperate.

FDIC insured:

The Federal Deposit Insurance Corporation (FDIC) insures the total balances of bank accounts up to the maximum amount allowed by law.

Federal Housing Administration (FHA):

The FHA is part of the Department of Housing and Urban Development (HUD). It provides mortgage insurance and establishes construction and underwriting standards.

FICO Score:

FICO is a credit-scoring system (developed by the Fair Isaac Corporation) used by many credit-reporting agencies and creditors. FICO credit scores range from 300 to 850. Bankers, lenders, creditors, insurers, and retailers use many different credit-scoring formulas. The methods reach slightly differing results, because each scoring system evaluates credit data differently.

Finance Charges:

Finance charges are the cost of consumer credit expressed as a dollar amount. They include any charges, such as interest and fees, paid by a consumer to a creditor for obtaining a loan.

Finance Company:

A finance company is a business that provides consumer loans, often to individuals who cannot qualify for credit at a credit union or bank. Usually, the interest rates charged by a finance company are higher than those charged by other creditors.

Financial Health:

Your financial health is your overall financial situation.

Financial Institution:

Financial institutions use their funds primarily to purchase financial assets, such as deposits, loans, and securities. They include savings banks, capital-investment firms, and insurance companies.

Fixed Expenses:

A fixed expense is one that remains relatively constant from period to period. Examples are rent payments, mortgage payments, and food.

First Mortgage:

A first mortgage is the primary loan on real property. It has priority over all secondary mortgages.

Fixed Rate:

An interest rate that remains constant for the duration of a loan or credit-card authorization.

Fixed-Rate Option:

A fixed-rate option allows the borrower to convert a variable-rate home-equity loan to a fixed rate one in order to lock in a fixed monthly payment and term.

Fixed-Rate Mortgage (FRM):

This is a mortgage with an interest rate that remains constant for the full duration of the loan. Fixed-rate mortgages have longer terms (15-30 years) and higher interest rates than adjustable-rate mortgages but are not subject to the risk of changing interest rates.

Foreclosure:

A foreclosure is a proceeding in which a lender reclaims real property because of the borrower's failure to pay according to the terms of the lending agreement.

Fraud:

Fraud is the intentional misrepresentation, concealment, or omission of the truth in order to deceive someone for personal gain. Examples are identity theft and illegal e-mail schemes.

Fraud Alert:

A fraud alert is a process whereby individuals who suspect identity theft may request that the credit bureaus place a 90-day fraud alert on their credit-reports. Identity-theft victims can request that longer fraud alerts (up to seven years) be placed on their credit-report records.

Front-End Ratio:

The front-end ratio is the percentage of your monthly pretax income that can reasonably be applied toward a house payment. Lenders use it as one factor in determining whether a potential buyer can afford to buy a home. Many experts feel your front-end ratio should not exceed 28 percent.

Forbearance:

Forbearance is a method of postponing loan payments for a temporary period and is granted by a lender to allow a borrower to catch up with delinquent payments. Interest accrues during the forbearance period regardless of whether the loan is subsidized or unsubsidized and is added to the loan balance. Forbearance is common among unemployed former students with outstanding student loans.

Funds Transfer:

Also called a wire transfer, a funds transfer is the internal movement of funds between accounts in one bank and the external movement of funds between banks.

G

Garnishment:

Garnishment is the process of deducting money from an employee's salary in order to repay a delinquent debt. It can only be done with a court order.

Good-Faith Estimate:

The Real Estate Settlement Procedures Act (RESPA) requires lenders and brokers to provide each customer with a good-faith estimate of the fees and costs that are associated with the loan.

Grace Period:

If you do not have an outstanding revolving balance on your credit card, the grace period is the interest-free period between the date of purchase and the date that the expenditure appears on your credit-card statement (typically 25 days). With most credit-card accounts, the grace period applies only if you pay your balance in full each month.

Guarantor:

A guarantor is a person or legal entity that makes a guaranty.

Guaranty:

A guaranty is an agreement in which one person assumes the responsibility to perform a specific act or duty for another.

H

Hard Inquiry:

A hard inquiry is an item on a credit report that indicates that an individual or entity has requested a copy of the report. Potential creditors make hard inquiries when you apply for credit. Hard inquiries appear on your credit report and are detrimental to your credit score.

Home Equity:

Home equity is the portion of a home's value that the borrower owns outright. This is the difference between the fairmarket value of the home and the principal balances of all mortgage loans.

Household Income:

Household income is income from all sources including wages, commissions, bonuses, alimony, child support, social-security benefits, retirement benefits, unemployment compensation, disability payments, dividends, and interest.

HUD:

The U.S. Department of Housing and Urban Development.

I

Independent Bank:

An independent bank (community bank) is a locally owned and operated commercial bank that derives its funds from, and lends its money to, the community in which it operates.

Individual Taxpayer Identification Number (ITIN):

The Internal Revenue Service issues an ITIN to taxpayers who do not have social-security numbers. The number can be used to apply for credit and loans or to access credit reports. Typically, an ITIN has nine digits.

Income Verification:

Banks today insist on verification, via documentation, of a prospective applicant's income.

Inquiry:

An inquiry is an item on your credit report that states that someone with a permissible purpose under Fair-Credit-Reporting-Act (FCRA) regulations has requested a copy of your credit-report data. (See Soft Inquiry, Promotional Inquiry, and Hard Inquiry.)

Installment Account (Installment Loan):

An installment account is a loan that you promise to pay back by paying equal amounts of money on a regular basis, usually monthly, for a specific amount of time. Examples include personal, merchant, and automobile loans. Although mortgage loans are also considered to be installment accounts, the credit-reporting agencies usually classify them as real-estate accounts.

Interchange Fee:

An interchange fee is an additional fee charged by an ATM (automated-teller machine) owner against another institution whose customer has used its terminal. Such fees vary by type of transaction activity.

Interest:

The interest rate that a bank or credit issuer charges for the money it lends to you. Interest is calculated as a percentage of the money borrowed.

Interest-Only Loan:

An interest-only loan is structured to allow the borrower to pay back only the interest on the principal balance, leaving the principal balance unchanged. At the end of the interest-only term, the borrower has several options, to include paying the principal or converting the loan to an amortized one. Interest-only loans are usually short-term and are structured so that the borrower can take advantage of rising real-estate prices. They have fallen out of favor with the development of the current credit crisis.

Interest Rate:

The rate that a lender charges for the money it lends to you. For variable-rate-credit-card plans, the interest rate is explicitly tied to some other interest rate. The interest rate on fixed-rate-credit-card plans can also change over time, but they must remain within the boundaries of the agreement.

Interest-Rate Cap:

This is a limit on how much the interest rate or monthly payment can change at certain times (rate-adjustment periods) or over the life of the loan. Interest-rate caps are used for adjustable-rate mortgages where the interest rates can vary.

Internet Banking:

Financial services accessed via the Internet's Worldwide Web.

Introductory Rate:

This is a low interest rate for a short duration offered by credit-card companies to attract new customers. Be careful, though, because if you make a late payment during the reduced-interest period, the special interest rate may be revoked or terminated, depending upon the offer.

J

Joint Account:

A joint account is one that is shared by two or more people. Each joint-account holder is legally responsible for the debt, and the account will be reported on each individual's credit report.

Judgment:

A judgment is a legal decision made by a court in a civil action after a creditor files suit against a defaulting borrower. It typically requires that the defendant (debtor) deliver an amount of money to the plaintiff (creditor) to satisfy a debt or pay a penalty. Judgments are harmful to your credit scores. They remain on your credit reports for seven years.

Junk Bond:

A junk bond is a form of bond that, because of its low credit rating or lack of credit rating, is considered a high-risk investment and consequently carries a high interest rate.

L

Late Payment (Delinquent Payment):

A failure to deliver a payment on or before the time agreed. If you miss the due date, the account is considered past due, and you may be charged a late fee. Late payments harm your credit scores and remain on your reports for seven years.

Late-Payment Fee:

A late-payment fee is an additional fee or penalty charged by a creditor or lender when a payment is late.

Lender:

A lender is an individual or financial institution that provides a loan to a borrower.

Liability:

Liability is the responsibility of a cardholder for a loan or credit account. When applying for credit, a cardholder agrees to be responsible for any charges to the account, including purchases, fees, and finance charges.

Lien:

This is a legal claim placed on your property by a business or person to whom you owe a debt. Usually, liens are filed against property when a debt is unpaid beyond its due date. They can create severe problems for property owners. The property against which the lien has been recorded cannot be sold until the issue is resolved, and tax liens can remain on your credit report indefinitely.

Letter of Credit:

A document issued by a lending institution on behalf of a buyer stating the amount of credit the buyer has available and that the lending institution will honor drafts written by the buyer up to that total.

Limited Appreciation:

This is a restriction on the amount of appreciation that a property owner can realize at a point-of-sale of the property.

Loan:

A loan is a transaction wherein an owner of property, called a lender, makes an agreement with another party, called a borrower, to use or purchase the lender's property. The borrower customarily promises to pay for the property in a timely, predetermined manner along with interest. When the property is cash, the document used to effect the borrower's promise is called a promissory note.

Loan Guarantee:

A loan guarantee is a program offered by some state and federal agencies that decreases a lender's risk by guaranteeing a portion of a debt against default. Loan guarantees apply to real-estate loans and target projects that offer a public benefit but are considered too risky to finance privately.

Loan-Origination Fee:

A loan-origination fee is a charge for opening a new loan. It is one of several fees you may encounter when securing a loan. In real-estate transactions, it is often paid through "points."

Loan-Processing Fee:

A lender may charge a loan-processing fee for accepting a loan application and processing the supporting paperwork.

Lock Period:

This is the time during which a lender guarantees a specific interest rate. The lender guarantees the interest rate for a period of time, typically 30 to 60 days, to give the borrower an opportunity to complete some activity.

Lock-In:

This is a lender's written agreement guaranteeing an interest rate to the purchaser of real estate, but only if the loan is closed within a specific period of time.

Low-Documentation Loan:

This is a mortgage that requires less verification of income and/or assets than a conventional loan. Low-documentation loans are primarily intended for entrepreneurs and self-employed borrowers.

Low-Down Mortgage:

This is a secured loan that permits a lower-than-normal down payment. Lenders offer low-down mortgages to firemen, police officers, military personnel, and others.

M

Margin:

The number of percentage points a lender adds to the index value of a loan to calculate the adjustable-rate-mortgage interest rate at each adjustment period, with a point equaling one percent of that index.

Maturity Date:

The term "maturity date" refers to the date when the principal amount of a debt becomes due and payable. It also refers to the date on which a loan must be repaid.

Merged-Credit Report:

This report merges your credit-history data from the three credit-reporting agencies (TransUnion, Equifax, and Experian). The information is displayed in a side-by-side format for easy comparison. AnnualCreditReport.com (www.annualcreditrport.com) offers this style of reporting once a year.

Minimum Payment:

The lowest payment toward an account you can deliver by the due date while still meeting the terms of your loan or credit-card agreement.

Mortgage:

This is a legal document that acts as a lien on a property as security for the repayment of a loan by a borrower.

Mortgage Loan:

A mortgage loan utilizes a mortgage to secure a loan with real property .

Mortgage Banker:

A person or company that originates home loans, sells them to investors, and processes the monthly payments.

Mortgage Broker:

A mortgage broker is an individual or company that matches lenders with borrowers and receives payment for its services, but does not make loans directly (as would a mortgage banker).

Mortgage Refinancing:

Mortgage refinancing is the process a borrower uses to pay off and replace an existing loan with a new mortgage. Borrowers usually do it to obtain lower interest rates and lower monthly payments.

N

Negative Amortization:

This occurs when the debt balance of your loan increases each month because your monthly payments are inadequate to cover the interest and principle charged.

National Foundation for Consumer Credit (NFCC):

A nonprofit organization dedicated to educating consumers regarding the wise use of credit. The NFCC serves as an umbrella company for a group of consumer-credit-counseling-service offices throughout the nation.

Nontaxable Income:

Money you earn which is not taxed by federal, state, or local government. This money can come from a variety of sources, including disability pay and legal settlements.

O

Obligation:

The requirement of a debtor to pay a debt.

Opt-Out:

Short for "option out," this government-sponsored service allows you opt out of pre-approved-credit-card offers, insurance offers, and other third-party-marketing offers. The telephone number to call for this service is 1-888-5-OPTOUT. Calling it will assist you in stopping all regular-mail offers that use credit-report information obtained from the three national credit-reporting agencies.

Outstanding Balance:

The total amount of money that you owe on a loan.

Over-Limit Fee:

An additional charge imposed on you by a creditor when your spending exceeds the credit limit of your credit card.

Owner Financing:

This term refers to a real-estate sale transaction in which the seller of the property provides some or all of the financing.

P

Penalty Rate:

This refers to the higher interest rate you must pay if you make one or more late payments on a credit-card account. The amount of the penalty rate is set in the credit-card agreement and can increase the interest payable by several percentage points. A card issuer can also impose a penalty rate if the consumer maintains a balance that is too high.

Points:

Points are fees that a borrower pays to a mortgage lender at the closing of a real-estate transaction. Two types of points exist—origination and discount. In both cases, one point is equivalent to one percent of the mortgage loan. If you borrow $300,000, for example, a point would be $3,000.

Pre-Approval Letter:

This is a non-binding decision, based on a cursory review of your credit history and sent to you in the form of a letter from a lender or broker, that estimates how much you can borrow. It can apply to a real-estate loan, a credit-card application, or a credit-line offer that is pre-approved based upon available data without further information supplied by you. Although a real-estate pre-approval letter might be useful for securing a loan, a pre-approved-credit-card offer is another matter. You should beware of the latter.

Predatory Lending:

Predatory lending occurs most commonly in loans for the purchase of motor vehicles. It often involves making high-cost loans based on the borrower's assets rather than the ability to repay the obligation or inducing the borrower to refinance a loan repeatedly in order to charge points and fees each time the loan is refinanced. Predatory lenders often target individuals with poor credit histories.

Prepaid Credit Card:

Borrowers whose applications for credit cards are rejected because of poor credit frequently turn to prepaid credit cards to solve the obvious problem that hotels, car-rental companies, and airlines require major credit cards for making reservations. The borrower opens a prepaid-credit-card account by depositing funds with the card issuer, similar to depositing money in a checking account.

Prepayment:

This is when a borrower pays a portion or the entire amount of the principal of a loan before the due date. Frequently, lending agreements provide that prepayment will reduce the total amount of interest that the borrower must pay.

Prepayment Penalty:

A prepayment penalty is a fee charged by a lender to a borrower who makes a prepayment. At the time of negotiation of the lending agreement, you should insist that all prepayment penalties be deleted from the contract. When the lender's representative presents you with the corrected version of the contract, be sure to read it carefully to ensure that the clause was indeed taken out.

Pre-Qualification Letter:

Pre-qualification letters are similar to but less formal than pre-approval letters. Lenders often use them in mass-marketing strategies with the intention of luring people with less-than-perfect credit.

Previous Balance:

The term "previous balance" refers to the total account balance due at the end of the last billing cycle.

Prime Rate:

The prime rate is the interest rate that major banks charge to their best corporate customers. Each bank sets it own prime rate, although because the market is so competitive, most of the time the rate is the same at all banks.

Principal:

The principal is the original amount of money borrowed. With respect to credit cards, the principal represents the price of purchased items or the amount of a cash advance.

Promissory Note:

A written promise made by a person (maker) to pay a certain sum of money to another person (payee). It also lists the maker's and payee's rights and responsibilities under the loan agreement, including how and when the loan must be repaid.

Promotional Inquiry:

A promotional inquiry is an inquiry into a limited portion of your credit history without your knowledge or consent. Legitimate lenders (such as credit-card companies) that are trying to entice you with a pre-approved offer are the most-frequent users of promotional inquiries. Fortunately, these inquiries are considered "soft" and do not damage your credit score.

Public Records:

Public records are often viewed to be one of the most important aspects of your credit report. A tax lien, bankruptcy, or civil lawsuit can remain on your credit report for seven to ten years.

Q

Quarterly:

In financial calculations, the term "quarterly" refers to a way of dividing a year into three-month intervals. For example, the first quarter in a calendar year is January through March, the 2nd is April through June, the 3rd is July through September, and the 4th is October through December. For accounting purposes, businesses and other organizations often use a fiscal year instead of a calendar year, so that periods of accelerated business activity, such as Christmas, do not interfere with their year-end accounting work.

R

Rate:

This refers to the annual rate of interest on a loan and is typically expressed as a percentage.

Rate Cap:

For an adjustable-rate-mortgage, the rate cap is a limit on how much the interest rate can change during a period of time, either at each adjustment period or over the life of the loan.

Rate Lock-In:

When granting a rate lock-in, the lender guarantees the borrower a specified interest rate, provided the loan closes by a certain date. Always get a rate lock-in agreement in writing.

Rate Shopping:

Applying for credit with several lenders in an attempt to obtain the best interest rate for a loan is common practice and is known as rate shopping.

Re-aging Accounts:

Re-aging is part of the credit-report-dispute process and means that the creditor agrees to correct an erroneous late-payment statement on your credit report. Unfortunately, re-aging is also sometimes used illegally by collection agencies to make debt accounts appear younger than they are. Collection accounts that appear to be active are still collectible.

Repayment Period:

The repayment period is the amount of time you have to pay off your loan.

Rebate:

Rebates usually consist of cash given back to you by the seller or lender. Of course, you are receiving your own money. Unscrupulous lenders use rebates to hide exorbitant interest rates or to cover abusive closing costs, so you should proceed with caution. Loans with rebates often carry higher interest rates than loans with points. The best loans, of course, are those with low interest rates, no rebates, and no points.

Repossession:

This is the act of taking property from a borrower as a result of an inability or unwillingness to pay a debt on time.

Revolving Account:

A revolving account allows for flexibility in the balance and monthly-payment amount. Most credit cards are revolving accounts; most home loans are not.

Refinancing:

Refinancing is the process of using a new loan (generally extended at a lower interest rate) to pay off an existing one.

Residential Mortgage Credit Report (RMCR):

This report utilizes information from at least two of the three national credit bureaus, in addition to the information you provide on your loan application.

Risk Score:

This is an alternative term for credit score. A credit score is a statistical system for assigning numerical values to characteristics related to information in your credit report. It usually ranges from 300 to 850, with 680 or higher considered a good credit score. Many different credit-scoring formulas exist, and each one produces scores that vary slightly from those of the other credit-reporting agencies.

S

Savings Bank:

These are depository banks that focus primarily on consumer-savings deposits.

Scoring Model:

A scoring model is an algorithm that evaluates the risk you represent to the lenders. It views your past spending habits in an attempt to predict your future behavior. Many scoring systems exist to generate credit scores, which means that your credit scores are likely to be different on the three major credit-bureau reports. I recommend that you obtain your credit-report information from all three of them.

Second Mortgage:

A second mortgage is a loan that is subordinate to another loan on the same piece of property. Homeowners often use second mortgages to obtain funds for home improvements and sometimes to start businesses. This secondary loan often has a different interest rate from the first and can originate with a completely different lender.

Secured Credit Card:

If you deposit $2,000 in a bank and then apply for a credit card with a $2,000 limit from that bank, the card is secured because the bank has the collateral it needs to be assured you can pay off whatever debt you occur on the card. For obvious reasons, secured credit cards are easier to obtain than standard credit-card accounts. They can be extremely helpful for borrowers with poor credit or no credit, and paying them back on time helps rebuild credit scores.

Secured Debt:

This is a debt for which repayment is guaranteed through collateral property of equal or greater value than the amount of the original loan. If the debtor does not pay, the issuer may take possession of the collateral. A home mortgage is an example of a secured debt. If the borrower fails to repay the loan, the lender may foreclose and repossess the home in lieu of payment.

Settlement:

In the world of credit, settlement refers to an agreement a borrower reaches with a creditor to pay a debt for less than the total amount owed. While this might sound beneficial to the borrower, it has a downside. Settlements are listed on your credit history and can count against your credit score.

Social-Security Number (SSN):

The U.S. government assigns a nine-digit number to each American citizen for the purpose of tracking social-security savings and benefits. Creditors, lenders, banks, insurers, hospitals, and employers also use the information. Unfortunately, in the hands of identity thieves, your social-security number can be used to steal money and good credit. You should use extreme caution when divulging your social-security number, and if at all possible, you should avoid doing so over the Internet or telephone.

Soft Inquiry:

A soft inquiry is a form of inquiry allowed by the three national credit-reporting agencies that does not harm your credit score. Soft inquires are recorded when business access your credit history and information for purposes other than the processing of loan applications. Most pre-approved-credit offers result from this type of inquiry.

Stated Income:

Some lenders require only that applicants state their sources of income without providing supporting documentation. Most banks stopped this practice when the credit-and-housing crisis erupted in 2007.

Sub-Prime Borrower:

If your credit score is from 560 to 679, you are considered a sub-prime borrower and will likely pay higher interest rates on your loans. Sub-prime borrowers can qualify for loans and credit, but usually must pay higher interest rates or comply with special terms. The recent lending crisis occurred in part because hungry lenders wooed too many sub-prime borrowers who were unable to pay back the loans as housing prices dropped and balloon payments became due.

T

Term:

This is the period of time that spans the life of a loan.

Tradeline:

An official term for most of the accounts listed on your credit reports. Each account is listed separately, and the listing is called a tradeline.

TransUnion:

One of three national credit-reporting agencies that collect and sell consumer-credit-history records to banks and lenders.

Truth-in-Lending Act of 1968 (TILA):

This is a federal law requiring the disclosure of credit terms by lenders in a standard format. Intended to facilitate comparisons of the lending terms used by different financial institutions, it allows consumers to make loan decisions easier.

U

Unknown Account (UN):

An unknown account is an account of an unknown loan type.

Universal Default Clause:

A universal default clause is an anti-borrower contract provision that allows a creditor to increase your interest rates when you make a late payment on **any** account, not just on its account. It is simply another method used by credit-card companies to force you to pay your bills on time.

Unsecured Debt:

Unsecured debt is debt for which no collateral is required. An example is a credit-card account. Most borrowers must have a prime credit score (680 or above) to obtain an unsecured account.

V

Variable Rate:

The interest rate on this form of adjustable-rate loan can go up or down and is usually tied to the national prime rate. A variable-rate loan differs from a fixed-rate one for which you pay a set interest rate throughout the life of the loan.

Y

Yield:

The amount of interest or profit accrued by a loan or investment during a specified time.

Z

Zoom:

What your credit scores and financial capabilities will do once you start utilizing the tools we've provided in *Recreditpair*. I want you to zoom to the top, where you belong.